Endorsements for *Relevant Acts*

Kevin's style is conversational and his thought patterns are easy to follow. Kevin addresses a very important question which so many pastors struggle with; they are afraid of the Holy Spirit. What is needed is solid teaching: this is a wonderful, instructive book on the need, presence and working of the Holy Spirit. Kevin's multiple scriptural references bring authority to the text; his personal stories are so real (we've all been there); his testimonies illuminate the teaching and make it practical. I believe this book will be a "life changer" in the ministry of many pastors. Congratulations on a great work.

Gary Blanchard,
Assistant Superintendent of the Assemblies of God, Illinois District

This book addresses how a Pastor can have a growing, vibrant church without excluding or quenching the Holy Spirit. I highly recommend this book.

Dr. Leon van Rooyen
Founding President of Global Ministries & Relief, Inc.

A great read—provocatively challenging, concise and thought provoking.

Andy Elmes
Senior Pastor, Family Church and Founder of Synergy Alliance and
Synergy Christian Churches

Relevant Acts

Relevant Acts

A DISCUSSION
ON THE SPIRIT
IN A MODERN AGE

KEVIN KRINGEL

Published in 2015 by Great Big Life Publishing
Empower Centre, 83-87 Kingston Road, Portsmouth, PO2 7DX, UK

British Library Cataloguing in Publication Data

A catalogue record for this book is available from the British Library

ISBN-13: 978-09928027-8-3
ISBN-10: 0992802784
eBook ISBN: 978-09928027-9-0

Dedication

I would like to dedicate this book to my church family. Life Church, you are the most supportive and passionate, visionary people any leader could ever hope for. Thank you for your belief in my family and God's call on our lives.

I would like to thank Jennifer Hale and Elise Wood for their many hours of editing and helping put this book together.

To my parents, thank you for teaching me to have a deep love for the things of God.

Finally to my wife Maria, and my children Isaiah, Kylie, Daniel and Gabriel. Thank you for all the hugs and kisses and words of encouragement with every big step I take. Your love and belief in my life makes me believe I can always climb higher. I love you.

I would like to truly dedicate this work to the Holy Spirit. I pray this book honors who He is and what He desires to accomplish in the church that He loves so much.

Kevin Kringel
Lead Pastor, Life Church

Contents

Foreword

O ver the last few years Kevin has become a very
good friend. My wife Gina and I have been blessed
and inspired watching him and his wife Maria lead Life
Church, a very healthy and vibrant multisite church
in Illinois. It is very much a God-centred church, very
deliberate about teaching and defending the central
truths of God's Word, and in training people to know
and experience God personally and to walk in His ways.

I've had the privilege to minister for Kevin and Maria
many times over the last few years and have always been
so encouraged by how they have managed to create an
atmosphere in their meetings that is modern, welcoming
and attractive, without losing the essence of the power
of God and the things of the Spirit. Getting this balance
right is something that is so needed in today's Church
especially in the West. From observing Kevin's ministry
it is clear he has spent time seeking God in regard to

this, and he has certainly found a good 'recipe' for doing it that is more than just a good theory—it truly works.

In *Relevant Acts* Kevin successfully captures his passion and wisdom for building a Spirit-filled church that causes lives to be transformed, not merely modified. This book makes for a great read for those who want more than just a 'modern church' with its comfort, lighting effects and programs; it is a very balanced nutritional meal for those hungry to know how to see the power of God naturally flowing again in the 21st century Church, and indeed their lives.

More than that this is a handbook for the person who desires to know more of God's power active and flowing in their everyday life. Its central theme is simple yet very profound, questioning what needs to be questioned and offering very well thought out conclusions for such questions as, "How do we make the powerful things we read about in the book of Acts relevant to the generation God has given us to serve?" It will cause you to answer other significant questions in your heart and thinking that need to be answered: "What place should the things of the Spirit have in the modern Church? What does a life flowing with spiritual gifts look and sound like?" Boldly Kevin asks, "Are we robbing people from things God has for them, thinking we are somehow protecting them?"

Kevin's ability to teach is very bespoke, using his unique

way of unpacking the truth of Scripture He will cause you to stop and think, to ponder, and then reach your own conclusions regarding how we can today make relevant the things that the Early Church did, and how we can know what was recorded in the book of Acts in our everyday lives.

Let me ask you a question: are you hungry to see the gifts of the spirit flowing again in your life and ministry? Have you become stuck in your understanding of how original church and modern church can experience the same when it comes to the things of God? Then dive into this inspiring read with a heart hungry to get revelation, not just knowledge, and I know without a doubt you will not be disappointed.

Well done, Kevin, for daring to answer real questions that real people are asking, and thank you for answering them in a way that people can understand and daily apply.

Love you, my friend, may this book empower and equip the lives of many.

Andy Elmes

Introduction

The catalyst to this book hit me during an interview I was holding with a very intelligent, up-and-coming pastor. As an executive presbyter in my state, I hold interviews for pastors who are taking the next step toward becoming licensed with the Assemblies of God in our region. During one particular session, the pastor we were interviewing was asked about his beliefs regarding the Holy Spirit. He paused, and seemed to question how to respond appropriately. When he answered, he spoke truthfully, and his comment captured what I believe to be the growing concern of many people, especially church leaders and young church planters. I don't remember his answer word for word, but his statement went something like this: "I believe in the Holy Spirit, but I fear that if I *really* had a Holy Spirit type church, it would mean that I would be destined to have a small, unappealing, and culturally irrelevant church."

This man was reluctantly revealing his true fear: that he would have to choose between the Holy Spirit and having a church that would thrive and grow. He was battling an idea that said, "If you open the doors to one, you will have to sacrifice the other." I really appreciated his honesty, but in that instant, I also realized that this pastor was expressing a feeling that was present in many peoples' lives. This belief has spread its way into the hearts of current believers everywhere, and it is quickly becoming the dominant perspective of the next generation of church leaders.

The average church attendee may feel that to lead a true and unashamed life led by the Holy Spirit, he or she may have to choose between being a successful business person, a thriving politician, an admired doctor, a flourishing entrepreneur, or a Spirit-filled "nut job". Somehow we have placed the Holy Spirit in the "crazy box". It's as if we think that anyone who leads a real, Spirit-filled life is out of touch. We think that a Spirit-filled person's head is in the clouds, that he or she is merely a thrill-seeker, and that those who claim to be led by the Spirit are not effective movers or influencers on the earth.

However, I'd like to take a moment to testify about my own life and church. As of 2015, I am under forty years of age, so I fall into the category of an up-and-coming leader. In the past eleven years, the Lord has allowed me to take a church of eighteen people and grow it into a multi-site church. Our main campus has over 1,000 people on a weekly basis, and we meet in a small, rural town in Illinois with a population of just over 10,000 people. We've planted two other churches besides our own during this time, and we just recently began airing on television. Currently, **we average over 20,000 viewers on a weekly basis.**

I am unashamedly filled with the Holy Spirit. I believe we have seen great success in our church, and I believe we will continue to see God move. Of course, I realize that this success is not due to my own abilities; it is due to the leading of God's Spirit, to His presence, and to His power touching people in miraculous ways. Prayerfully, our story can help put to rest the question of whether or not churches have to choose between being Spirit-filled and being "successful."

It is important to understand that mere numbers have never determined success in God's eyes. Our success as individuals is determined by our trust in and obedience to a gracious and loving heavenly Father. If you've obeyed Him, you have succeeded, despite the size of your congregation. Sure, we are each gifted and talented, and we can always build something without the help of God's Spirit. However, when we try to operate a ministry on our own, the extent of our influence is capped. Our ministry will hit a certain limit and then cease to grow. Without the Spirit of God, we are limited to our own potential, but with the influence of the Holy Spirit, our effectiveness in ministry is limitless.

Please do not oversimplify the definition of a Spirit-led church. This book is not a simple discourse on whether or not tongues should be in the Church. The Holy Spirit's presence in the Church is about so much more than that; His presence is about abilities. It is about *His* abilities, which go beyond our own human talent. In Christ's Church, there is always His "super" on our "natural," which makes us supernatural people. His gifts, wisdom, abilities, and powers are all brought together in a beautiful union when God's Spirit moves in God's Church, and the result is a thriving community.

This book is not only for pastors of spiritually hungry churches, but it is also for the believer who is eager to walk in the gifts and callings of God's Spirit. This book is a conversation. It is a "how to" book, and it is also a discussion about the Truth as we consider the Holy Spirit in our lives and churches. If we are honest, there has been a lot of confusion, and even abuse, when it comes to the Holy Spirit's activity in our churches and lives. The fact is—we need the presence and ability of the Holy Spirit more today than any generation before us. We have a whirlwind of books and opinions about Him, but so few churches and so few people really walk in practical power and relationship with God's Spirit. We debate His place and relevance in our Western churches. Rather than allowing the Holy Spirit to be Himself, we often try to fit Him into the boxes of our personal cultures and experiences.

If you know anything about the Bible, either Old or New Testament, you know that God isn't going to stay in a box. He never has. He was once "contained" in a box called the Ark of the Covenant and hidden behind a curtain, too holy to be reached. But that "box" was never intended to be His permanent residence. God had a plan. Jesus came down from heaven to earth, led a perfect life, fulfilled a perfect exchange, and changed absolutely everything. He destroyed the curtain of separation, and God left the "box" once and for all. Any previous boundaries between God and His children were eliminated then and there. He wants a relationship with his people, and He's not going back into any box or behind any curtain ever again!

God spoke to my heart one day about The Holy Spirit's role in our lives and the role He should take in our churches. The phrase that rang in my heart was, "the Holy Spirit is not simply *A* spirit from God; He is *THE* Spirit of God." It is important to understand that The Holy Spirit is not an angel or spirit sent *from* God. The Holy Spirit is God Himself. God sent

HIMSELF to be our Helper in our everyday lives. The Holy Spirit did not reserve Himself for Sunday morning church services only. (Thank God for that!)

We see this pattern throughout the Bible. The book of Acts is overflowing with great encounters between God and His people through the person and work of the Holy Spirit. Most of these encounters did not happen solely at designated church services or particular altar times. They were real encounters in the lives of real people that took place in homes, on the streets, and in places where people lived normal, everyday lives. When we begin to understand these things, we can then begin to see His undeniable relevance. Then, we will come to see and know the need to teach this generation about Him once again.

> *And you know that God anointed Jesus of Nazareth with the Holy Spirit and with power. Then Jesus went around doing good and healing all who were oppressed by the devil, for God was with him.*
> **Acts 10:38, NLT**

We can see the purpose and power upon the believer's life in this passage—that the believer may be equipped to "do good" and "heal those oppressed of the devil."

The Holy Spirit was sent to assist us in the destiny of our lives. It is a real disappointment that we've limited

Him to a few shouts in a church service or a certain type of manifestation that we may have seen in a revival service years ago. He is God, and He has a mission to see both you and those lost in this world saved, restored, overcoming, and effective.

It is my prayer that this book inspires church leaders to be intentional about their congregations' relationships with the Spirit of God. As a leader, it is important to ask yourself these questions: How am I introducing my people to the Holy Spirit? What do they believe about Him? How do they operate in His gifts? Is this just a display or the true power of God at work?

Church Leader, your sheep look to you to feed them. We must make sure the diet is balanced. I hope that this book inspires every believer, individual, and/ or church leader to be intentional about his or her relationship with the Holy Spirit.

Background

When I was a boy, my parents made a deal with God, and I can still remember it clearly. The deal was made when we visited a small, local Assemblies of God church. My parents told God that if He would give them their dream home, they would continue attending church faithfully. To make a long story short, we ended up getting the home, and my family started attending Lighthouse Assembly of God in Riverside, California.

I was only eight years old at the time, but the decision to bring our family to church changed my life forever. Like any other eight-year-old, I would have preferred to stay home on Sunday mornings and watch cartoons, but my parents made a commitment they were determined to keep. As our family became increasingly involved in church, my mom soon became the choir director, and I inevitably ended up as a choir member.

It was in this little Spirit-filled church that I first understood the need for salvation—giving my life to Jesus Christ by asking Him into my heart. I was also introduced to the power of God through the reality of His Holy Spirit. I only vaguely remember bits and pieces about that church from my childhood. However, I distinctly remember attending the Sunday night services. The people who attended those services would relax and be themselves in the presence of God. Elderly ladies would stand up and share testimonies about healings or supernatural provision, and young men would share how God delivered them from addictions or past sins. At first, I paid little attention to the messages or testimonies. I would often pass the time by coloring on tithe envelopes or slowly drifting off to sleep while my mom gently tickled my arm.

It wasn't until one Sunday morning that the Lord got a hold of my life. At the end of the service, I went down to the altar and submitted my young heart to

Jesus. I was still too young to have committed any life-altering sins, but the moment I encountered God, I felt as if the weight of eternity itself was on my shoulders. And when He received me as His own, I felt clean, and I felt happy.

Some time after my salvation experience, a guest evangelist came to a Sunday night service and began to speak of the "filling" and "baptism" in the Holy Spirit. I was young with childlike faith, so I never questioned his theology about the Spirit of God. Why would I? I was simple-minded enough to think, "God has something more to give me; I want it!" Eight-year-olds don't debate receiving gifts; they just accept them.

I remember going up to the evangelist after service and asking if I could receive the Holy Spirit too. He was kind, but he was also in a hurry to go out with the pastor. He politely prayed for me and told me to repeat some words after him. Then He told me I was filled, gave me a little booklet, and said to go home, read it, and continue praying everything he taught me. As I read, I didn't *feel* anything, but I trusted the word of that evangelist. Moments later, I began speaking in a language that I had never learned. That was a game-changing moment for me.

After that encounter with God in my bedroom, I can truthfully say that I was forever changed. A boldness and a determination rose up within me to see others receive Christ. I began to step out boldly in faith, sharing the love of Christ with my friends in my small elementary school. Honestly, my school bus was a huge mission field; kids on the bus rides to and from school shared dirty comic strips, shouted profanity, and had inappropriate conversations about sex. Yet, in the middle of all this, I remember unabashedly drawing the attention of the kids around me to a rainbow that I saw out the window. I told them that this rainbow was a sign from God that He would never destroy the earth by a flood again. I was determined to speak God's Word, and no one had to tell me to be bold. Boldness just came naturally. More than that, an awareness of my responsibility to serve the world came over me. Life was no longer about me going to heaven; it was about the people I could bring with me.

As I look back, I am so grateful that I met the Holy Spirit at a young age because I never learned to doubt Him. My childhood was filled with services in which people would be miraculously healed, begin praying in a language they hadn't learned, dance before the Lord, and even fall to the ground under the presence of God. I can remember watching the precious older ladies in the congregation wave their paper fans during service. (I think the original intent of the fans was to cool them off when the church got too hot, but they soon became instruments of praise.) Each of the fans had a picture of Jesus with a sheep on one side, so when things got really exciting, you could see Jesus and sheep popping up everywhere. I even remember doing "Jericho marches," when both young and old would form a line and march around the sanctuary singing, dancing, and celebrating God's goodness.

These were good times, though I'm sure that had I been older, I would have raised an eyebrow at a few of the things that transpired. I'm sure there were extremes. There were possibly even manufactured moments when people operated purely out of emotion. Regardless, I am so grateful to have been introduced to the Holy Spirit at the very beginning of my walk with Christ. I am thankful that I wasn't "kept" or "protected" from Him, and as I've grown up, I have had to determine what is biblical, what is cultural, what is real, and what is false. I have evaluated what is healthy and what is abusive, and today, I can say I am much better off having received the Spirit as part of my core belief system.

It is my journey with the Holy Spirit that compels me to write this book. I want to have an open conversation about the Spirit of God. Let's be intentional about our beliefs regarding Him. Future churches and future generations of believers are at stake. Will we continue to ignore the Spirit for fear of abuse? When will we address the reasons why we've turned people off to the precious Spirit of God? Will our future be one that we deem as "safe," or will it be one in which God is again free to be the Head of His Church?

Remember, the Holy Spirit is not just another spirit from God; He is THE Spirit of God. Who He is, how He chooses to operate, and what He sees as best for us are really *His* prerogative. After all, He created the Church, and it is He who fills the Church. The Church is His property. You can be at peace and know that you can trust your faithful God. Once we understand that God the Father, God the Son, and God the Holy Spirit are one, then we can also trust the Holy Spirit to be as caring, relevant, accurate, and tender as Jesus or the Father Himself. You can know this and believe it. The Holy Spirit is not contrary to the Father and the Son; all three are one.

1

A Necessary Gift

There is a significant difference between needs and wants. It is physically impossible for human beings to survive without food, water, and shelter for an extended period of time. Therefore, human beings *need* food, water, and shelter. Wants, on the other hand, are desires that are not necessarily required to survive. Chocolate, for example, is a common desire, but a love of chocolate is only a love of chocolate. Of course, my wife may very well wish to debate this issue, but when she says she "needs" chocolate, she's really just saying that she would very much like some chocolate.

In the same way, just as our physical bodies require a few basic needs, we, as the body of Christ, require certain things in order to fulfill the Great Commission. In my opinion, Acts 2:38-39, which tells the story of the Day of Pentecost, reveals the two basic needs of the Church. Please keep in mind that when I speak of the "Church," I am not speaking of buildings or denominations. I'm speaking of those who have become a part of the body of Christ. The Church has always been composed of people; the buildings only exist to house those people.

> *Peter replied, "Each of you must repent of your sins and turn to God, and be baptized in the name of Jesus Christ for the forgiveness of your sins. Then you will receive the gift of the Holy Spirit. This promise is to you, and to your children, and even to the Gentiles—all who have been called by the Lord our God."*
> *Acts 2:38-39, NLT*

The two fundamental needs are these: Salvation and the gift of the Holy Spirit. Notice that Peter expresses more than just a need for salvation. Salvation includes the forgiveness of our sins, a real relationship with God, access to God, and eternal life, but Peter doesn't end with salvation. He brings up the Holy Spirit.

It's also important to notice that he describes the Holy

Spirit as a "gift." A gift, by definition, needs a giver and a receiver. So, who is giving this special gift and why?

*I (John the Baptist) baptize you with water, but **He** (Jesus) will **baptize you with the Holy Spirit!***
***Mark 1:8, NASB** (emphasis mine)*

*But **I will send you the Advocate**—the Spirit of truth. He will come to you **from the Father** and will testify all about me. And you must also testify about me because you have been with me from the beginning of my ministry.*
***John 15:26-27, NLT** (emphasis mine)*

*However, I am telling you nothing but the truth when I say it is profitable (good, expedient, advantageous) for you that I go away. Because if I do not go away, the Comforter (Counselor, Helper, Advocate, Intercessor, Strengthener, Standby) will not come to you [into close fellowship with you]; but if I go away, **I will send Him to you** [to be in close fellowship with you].*
***John 16:7, AMP** (emphasis mine)*

These verses reveal that the Holy Spirit is a gift sent by Jesus from God Almighty. Not only did Jesus send His Church this amazing gift, but He also became the one to baptize His people in the gift. In other words, the baptizer is not an evangelist, a pastor, or a denomination;

the baptizer is the Lord Himself.

Imagine this for a moment: Jesus prepares a gift. Jesus pays the price for the release of that gift, and then He makes you ready to be the vessel of that gift. Jesus is excited to give you the expression of the Godhead, someone who will fill you and equip you for maximum effectiveness, and so He offers you the gift.

Unfortunately, His people often say things like:

"I don't know if I really need that gift."

"I'd prefer not to have that gift."

"I'm scared by that gift."

"That gift is really unnecessary."

Can you picture the disappointment in His eyes as He hears these responses? His people have basically told Him that His gift is irrelevant or insignificant.

The filling and the baptism of the Holy Spirit come directly from the hands of our loving Savior, and I believe we can all agree that Jesus will never abuse you, damage you, or make you crazy. So, if Jesus places a high priority on this gift, it is a good idea to do the same thing.

Now keep in mind that though this baptism is called a gift, it is neither insignificant nor optional. In John 16:7, Jesus reveals the importance He places on the gift by stating that it would be better for His disciples that He go away. How difficult it must have been for the disciples to grasp such a concept! How could Jesus' departure from the world be more profitable than having Him around? But Jesus told them that He must leave so that the gift could come. How important and valuable this gift must be!

Jesus makes the need for this special gift evident by the priority and care He takes in administering it in the Bible. I will go into more detail on this later on, but phrases like "baptized," "filled," and "received" in relation to the Holy Spirit are all referencing this gift. People may think these words refer to different experiences, but these words are all speaking of the same empowering of the believer, an experience separate from salvation.

On the Day of Pentecost, Peter said that the gift of the Holy Spirit was for those listening that day, as well as for *everyone* whom the Lord would call throughout the generations of the church (Acts 2:39). Though I do not believe one needs this baptism experience to be saved or forgiven, each person who desires to be fully equipped to complete his or her destiny must have the baptism of the Holy Spirit.

I also believe this "baptism" is a truth that lasts as long as the Church is in this fallen world. Once we get to heaven and see everything clearly, some of these gifts may very well be outdated, but on this side of eternity, we need all the help the Helper is offering. We live in a fallen, hostile world. The enemy is using all kinds of physical and spiritual weapons to oppose the Kingdom of God, and we, as the Church, are supposed to be more than fully equipped. We do not have *just* enough to win; we have *more* than enough to win. It is through the Holy Spirit that we can be victorious over whatever other people, the enemy, or everyday life may throw our way.

> For **His divine power has bestowed upon us all things that [are requisite and suited] to life and godliness,** *through the [full, personal] knowledge of Him Who called us by and to His own glory and excellence (virtue).*
> **2 Peter 1:3, AMP** *(emphasis mine)*

> *But you shall receive power (ability, efficiency, and might) when the Holy Spirit has come upon you, and you shall be My witnesses in Jerusalem and all Judea and Samaria and to the ends (the very bounds) of the earth.*
> **Acts 1:8, AMP**

The Lord never intended for us to fulfill the Great Commission in our own strength. We were always meant to draw power from the Spirit of God, and the Spirit's power is not limited. His power comes from God Himself, which means that the power of God is dwelling in us through the person and work of the Holy Spirit.

The word for "power" used in Acts 1:8 is the Greek

word *dunamis*, which is the root of our English word for "dynamite" or "explosive power." In other words, God doesn't want His people to win barely; He wants His people to blow the competition away.

Note Paul's intentionality in Acts 19:

While Apollos was in Corinth, Paul went through the upper inland districts and came down to Ephesus. There he found some disciples. And he asked them, Did you receive the Holy Spirit when you believed [on Jesus as the Christ]? And they said, No, we have not even heard that there is a Holy Spirit.
Acts 19:1-2, AMP

He asked the disciples: "Have you received the Holy Spirit *since* you believed?" Again, this is referring to something that happens after the salvation experience. Paul wanted to make sure they were at maximum impact levels. He wasn't satisfied that they believed in Jesus; Paul wanted to be sure that they also received the promise of the Father, which is the gift of the Holy Spirit. Unfortunately, these disciples responded by saying, "We have not even heard that there is a Holy Spirit." I dearly hope we can avoid that same response in our generation. If we proclaim a message of salvation and leave out the gift of the Spirit, what will we have accomplished? In this situation, what you don't know *can* hurt you, or at least severely limit your walk as a believer.

> *My people are destroyed for lack of knowledge; because*
> *you [the priestly nation] have rejected knowledge, I will*
> *also reject you that you shall be no priest to Me.*
> **Hosea 4:6, AMP**

As church leaders, we truly are responsible for teaching, informing, and introducing all that God has made available to the body of Christ, even if it doesn't always make sense or feel necessary. *As leaders, we are not called to edit the Bible; we are called to preach it.* And to preach the gospel fully, the Bible declares that we need the Holy Spirit—His gifts and power.

> *They were convinced by the power of miraculous signs*
> *and wonders and by the power of God's Spirit. **In this***
> ***way, I have fully presented the Good News of Christ***
> *from Jerusalem all the way to Illyricum.*
> **Romans 15:19, NLT** *(emphasis mine)*

But what if the contemporary church is afraid of the Holy Spirit? What if they prefer to avoid the subject? What if the current trend is to believe, but not to practice, the moving of the Spirit?

Again, church leaders are not called to edit or determine

what is relevant. We are called to make these timeless, multicultural truths applicable in each generation, and if the present culture is ignorant of the Spirit, it is ultimately the fault of the Church.

I truly believe that most people today are not just *misinformed* about the Holy Spirit. They are also grossly *under-informed*. At our church in Illinois, we have hundreds of attendees from all walks of life and every denominational background. At times, some can appear almost illiterate about the things of the Spirit of God. After I preach a series on the Holy Spirit, people will often thank me and tell me that they have never before heard a message focused entirely on the Holy Spirit— who He is, why He's here, and how He operates in our lives. In other words, the message of the Holy Spirit needs to be delivered to the Church.

But how do we make the Holy Spirit relevant?

Relevancy is often where many people struggle because they fail to see the relevance of the Holy Spirit's power in their lives. Or, they consider His power limited to the activity of comfort or salvation. However, the power of the baptism of the Holy Spirit is one of the most relevant topics we can preach. His power goes beyond our natural means and helps us to be the victorious Body of Christ. The word "relevant" is defined as: *pertinent, applicable, related, significant, and important.* The Holy Spirit is *absolutely* relevant to our lives.

Just like we teach our children, we must also teach future generations the significance, importance, and relevance of the Holy Spirit in this generation. Those of you who are parents know that it is our responsibility to instill positive values and perspectives into our children. We have a role to play in teaching our children about the Holy Spirit, just like church leaders have a role in leading the Church.

Ask yourself this question: "How have I modeled the Holy Spirit to my children through my actions and words?" Are you showing your children a good example? Are you personally informed enough to teach them? Like any parent, I teach my children about honor, truth, God's love, and all things relevant to faith. I do not assume they will learn these things on their own or come to the right conclusion by themselves. I must help them see the relevance of these topics, and the same standard applies when I share messages on Sunday mornings. I always try to ask, "So what?" So what if there is a baptism? So what if there is an empowerment? How do these things affect me?

The issue today is not the Holy Spirit or His way of doing things. The real issue is that we as leaders have lost the ability to explain the relevance of the Holy Spirit and have forgotten to explain it to our churches. It is our job to make all Scripture applicable in the context of the modern world. The truth in the Bible is for all people and all generations. If truth is neglected, lost, or devalued, it's because of church leadership. The truth itself has not changed. As long as we walk in this life, we will always need God's real presence and power.

Please hear what I just said. We argue about the manner in which the Spirit is moving, but the real problem isn't with Him. The problem lies with us. We fail to understand or value parts of His identity. We fail to learn how to move in the power of the Spirit, but He is the same yesterday, today, and forever.

Of course, there are certain things that do lose relevance as culture advances, such as old telephone technology, old mailing methods, etc. However, the need for communication still remains. In the same way, some methods of presentation regarding the Holy Spirit may have changed, but the need for His communication and power have stayed the same. People are still sick, depressed, broken, disillusioned, and lost. Peoples' lives are still far from perfect. We still need help, healing, freedom, direction, correction, guidance, and to feel His presence in our lives. All of this demonstrates our need for the power of the Holy Spirit in this generation.

Another example occurs in Exodus as the Bible speaks of Israel's journey from Egypt to the Promised Land. During this journey, the Israelites end up walking through the Red Sea on their way to Canaan, but before they enter the Promised Land, they must also go through the Jordan River, yet another body of water. The Old Testament consistently foreshadows things to come, and the passing through the Red Sea can be seen as a foreshadowing of the need for baptism following salvation. Israel was in bondage. They were slaves under a harsh taskmaster named Pharaoh, and after the Israelites left their cruel taskmaster, a return to Egypt would only result in more bondage. The same is true in our own lives. Choosing to return to our old ways of living will result in our bondage; Christ has led us out of captivity and into freedom.

As the Israelites continued their journey, Moses made a declaration that God would one day raise up another prophet similar to himself—one who would lead His people out of bondage. Jesus was the ultimate fulfillment of that prophecy, and you can see many parallels between Moses and Jesus throughout the Bible. For example, King Herod, during the time of Jesus, decreed that all baby boys two years old and younger should be killed, and Pharaoh made that same decree when Moses was born.

The parallels continue as we see Moses leading Israel out from under the physical slavery of Pharaoh and into a life of freedom. In the same way, Jesus led us away from sin, bondage, and slavery and into a life of ultimate freedom. After leaving Egypt, the people of Israel passed through the Red Sea. God parted the waters, and as they walked through, they left their old taskmaster behind. As we go through or "under" the waters of baptism, we do the same thing. We walk away from sin and into our new lives of freedom, and this is why I believe so strongly in water baptism. Jesus commanded us to be baptized, and it's a great picture of freedom.

I could go on and on about the imagery of salvation and baptism within the story of Israel's Exodus from Egypt, but there is also important imagery in the story of the Jordan River. If the Exodus and the Red Sea are possible illustrations of our salvation and baptism experience, then what might the Jordan River symbolize? For years I had heard people sing of the parallel between crossing the Jordan and entering into heaven, but I realized one day that the crossing of the Jordan couldn't be speaking of the entrance into heaven. I'm inclined to think that heaven is a place of rest, and on the other side of the Jordan River, the Israelites faced battles, giants, and wars. So perhaps the crossing of the Jordan River was speaking of a different journey entirely.

It's also important to realize that the term "Promised Land" should not be applied exclusively to heaven. God promises a lot of things in this life, but all of His promises do not go unopposed. The enemy will often fight us, and he might even be occupying the land the Lord has promised us. For example, the enemy is involved in the world's system of finance, so if God has promised you a career or business success, you might have to engage in a few spiritual battles. You will need God's supernatural ability, wisdom, skill, and power to overcome and occupy your promise.

Your Promised Land is the promise about which God has spoken to you. For example, God also has a Promised Land called healing, but you might be facing the giant of sickness. Maybe your family, your body, or your business is your Promised Land. Regardless, we are called to bring down some spiritual strongholds (ideas/mindsets) and spiritual giants. Then, we will be empowered to build something in their place. In other words, Promised Lands can include more than just heaven; they can be places on this earth that God has given His people to occupy.

So, what was symbolic about the Israelites' trip over the Jordan River? Which baptism does it represent? I believe it speaks of the baptism of the Holy Spirit. Think about it for a moment. God's people are about to go into battle to take back land that was promised, and the story of the Jordan River speaks of an equipping. There was no way the Israelites could possess their Promised Land without going through the Jordan River.

And being assembled together with them, **He commanded them not to depart from Jerusalem, but to wait for the Promise of the Father,** *"which," He said, "you have heard from Me; for John truly baptized with water, but you shall be baptized with the Holy Spirit not many days from now.*

But you shall receive power when the Holy Spirit has come upon you; *and you shall be witnesses to Me in Jerusalem, and in all Judea and Samaria, and to the end of the earth."*

Acts 1:4-5, 8 *(emphasis mine)*

Here, Jesus is telling His disciples to go into the entire world and possess the Promised Land, but they had to go through a baptism to get ready for the task. It was that baptism which equipped them to take on the strongholds and giants they met along their journey.

Jesus would never tell us to do something He wasn't willing to do Himself. In the book of Joshua, **when the children of Israel crossed the Jordan, they were commanded to send the priests carrying the Ark of the Covenant first.** The Ark of the Covenant contained a copy of the Covenant, a jar filled with manna, and Aaron's staff, a dead rod which bloomed. All three of these things speak of Jesus—He is the fulfillment of the law, the bread from heaven, and life itself. The Ark is also often referred to as the mercy seat, which is where the blood necessary for the forgiveness of sins was sprinkled. And at the Jordan River, **the Ark went first**.

The Ark of the Covenant was the first to pass through the waters of baptism, thus preparing the way for the rest of us. In the New Testament, Jesus went through a baptism as well, but His baptism was not one of repentance. His baptism was a baptism of empowerment, and it took place in the same river through which the Ark of the Covenant passed.

It all took place at the Jordan River.

Jesus went into the Jordan River already in right relationship with God, but as He was baptized, He was endowed with the Holy Spirit, who descended on Him in the form of a dove. Jesus didn't need a "Red Sea" baptism. Notice that in the Gospels, Jesus' entire earthly ministry, including His miracles and toe-to-toe battles with the devil, occurred after this baptism. He was endued at that moment with the power to go and take the land His Father had promised Him. Jesus emptied Himself of His power and position when He came from heaven, and it wasn't until His baptism that He received the fullness of His power.

Let this same attitude and purpose and [humble] mind be in you which was in Christ Jesus: [Let Him be your example in humility:] Who, although being essentially one with God and in the form of God [possessing the fullness of the attributes

which make God], did not think this equality with God was a thing to be eagerly grasped or retained, **But stripped Himself [of all privileges and rightful dignity]**, *so as to assume the guise of a servant (slave), in that He became like men and was born a human being.*
Philippians 2:5-7, AMP *(emphasis mine)*

The power Jesus walked in was not inherent; it was from the baptism, the equipping of the Holy Spirit. That is why Jesus declared that we could do even greater works than His own. He told His disciples to wait for the same equipping to accomplish their assignments, and in this way, He demonstrated that the baptism of the Holy Spirit is necessary to carry out what God has called us to accomplish.

The Ark went first, and Jesus commanded us to go through the same waters. He prepared the way and showed us that this baptism wasn't about getting to heaven, but it was about bringing the Kingdom of Heaven to earth. And that same Holy Spirit, that same power who gave Jesus the ability to fulfill His assignment, is being offered to us. The baptism in the Holy Spirit is a necessary gift offered to every believer from the heart of God through the hands of Jesus.

2

The Bias

I have a friend who helped me navigate through the Holy Spirit discussion, a friend whom my wife and I consider to be a very close and trustworthy friend. She is a musician who has had the opportunity to minister to people of many different denominations, and as a result, she has obtained a perspective more broad than my own. One day, she visited our church while I was teaching on the Holy Spirit. During that particular message, I made the comment that I didn't see how people could be so afraid of the Spirit of God. I was unknowingly seeing things from only my perspective, and after the service, my friend kindly approached me. She explained that it wasn't really the *idea* of the Holy Spirit that drove people away; it was the *people* who claimed to be experts on the Holy Spirit who intimidated so many.

In that moment, I began to think about the people in our church who might be afraid of the Spirit of God. I realized that they were probably not against the doctrine of the Holy Spirit, but they may have experienced a negative encounter with someone who claimed to be led by the Holy Spirit. How many have been put off, offended, ridiculed, let down, or even abused by a "Spirit-filled" believer? How many have been hurt by someone claiming to minister in the name of the Holy Spirit? Maybe some people have become hesitant about the things of the Spirit in an effort to avoid becoming like the people who hurt them. It was after this realization that our church made it part of its mission to introduce people to an excellent, quality, and safe Holy Spirit environment.

Of course, it's not all that surprising that so many people have reacted to their negative experiences by forming negative biases. People develop opinions and belief systems in many different ways, and experiences are a common foundation. A bias can even be formed unknowingly, such as when parents honestly believe their child can do no wrong. Even when these parents are faced with proof that their child is not measuring up to their perceived levels of perfection, they can fail to see the facts. They have developed a bias that clouds their perception of reality. While it is natural for a parent to believe in the greatness of their child, it is not profitable to ignore the truth. Ignoring the truth will often keep their child from his or her destiny, and the same is true in our walk with the Lord. We must learn to embrace the truth, even when it disagrees with our personal beliefs.

It's sad to think that much of our culture looks at Spirit-filled believers as a type of trail mix—as flakes, fruits, and nuts. This common misconception may have come from personal experiences, training from mentors, information available, or a lack of information, but it is simply not the truth. There is a healthy way to approach the Holy Spirit, and it all starts with the Bible.

> *And so, brothers, select seven men who are well respected and **are full of the Spirit** and wisdom. We will give them this responsibility.*
> ***Acts 6:3, NLT** (emphasis mine)*

> *But Stephen, **full of the Holy Spirit**…*
> ***Acts 7:55a, NLT** (emphasis mine)*

> *Barnabas was a good man, **full of the Holy Spirit** and strong in faith. And many people were brought to the Lord.*
> ***Acts 11:24, NLT** (emphasis mine)*

It's clear that the apostles sought out leaders who were full of the Spirit of God. For example, the phrase "select those full of the Spirit" reveals that there is a tangible distinction between those who are filled and those who are not. In addition, the fact that the filling of the Spirit was a necessary qualification for leadership means that this tangible distinction was quite important. Being filled with the Spirit was a mark, a differentiating factor, and a necessity for leaders in the early Church. It was not enough to be forgiven and saved; it was imperative also to be filled.

In fact, all of our founding church leaders were Spirit-filled. All eleven of the remaining apostles were in the upper room when the tongues of fire appeared, including some of the leading ladies, such as the mother of Jesus herself. In 1 Corinthians 14:15-18, even Paul speaks of his relationship with the Holy Spirit. These are the very people who changed the face of the earth forever. It was from their writings and ministries that some of the world's greatest humanitarian efforts and social reforms were derived. It was from these Spirit-filled leaders that multiple countries built constitutions and economies. It was from their messages that beliefs regarding equal rights for women and children, young and old, slave and free, rich and poor all sparked revolutionary movements. In the beginning, "Spirit-filled" was not synonymous to "nut case"; it referred to a person who brought a life-changing message to the world. The word

"Spirit-filled" did not immediately bring to mind wild church services; the early church considered a Spirit-filled leader a world-changing leader.

I fear that church leaders have quit looking for Spirit-filled leaders to be our mentors or to fill the open positions on our church staffs. It's natural for us to look for "high level" leaders—those who have leadership skills, charisma, talent, verbal skills, and education. Of course, none of these qualities are wrong or bad to have. On the contrary, it's common sense to search for these qualities when building a solid team. But do we place enough of a priority on finding excellent Spirit-filled leaders who also possess these other natural skills? Why do we assume that a leader cannot have both? Unfortunately, there may not be many Spirit-filled leaders on this level available, which points to the problem we're discussing. Few are intentionally raising these types of leaders. Even though they may be harder to find right now, I believe a day will come when our generation will be filled with these excellent, high-level, Spirit-filled leaders. Do not give up the search as you staff your organization or look for Spirit-filled mentors. These leaders are out there; but you won't find them if you're not intentional in your search for them.

We need high-level leaders with a very real and active fellowship with the Holy Spirit. We need leaders who possess very precious and biblically excellent qualities. These leaders will be the ones heading the movements to feed the hungry, solve economic crises, stop human trafficking, educate the ignorant, and build cities out of devastation. These leaders will begin to change the perception of being Spirit-filled from "crazy" to "excellent." This generation needs Spirit-filled leaders who are not ashamed of their experiences and who are also well equipped in natural ability. It is these leaders who will bring the dimensions together, and God will use them as He puts His "super" on their "natural."

Still, there are those who believe that being filled with the Spirit is just simply unnecessary. Often, popular church leaders are described as "effective," "relatable," "talented," "hip," or "cool," but rarely are they ever described as "powerful." I get it. There was a generation in the past that valued being Spirit-filled above all else, and in their pursuit of the Spirit, they devalued common sense and knowledge. But we can't let that generation affect our entire perception of the Spirit.

I personally believe that if a leader is effective without the baptism/filling of the Spirit, then they can only be *more* effective when their natural abilities are combined with the Holy Spirit's creative, powerful, and supernatural ability. Imagine natural wisdom coupled with divine words of wisdom. Powerful, right?

Imagine serving in a business or a church with the gift of faith. Or imagine seeing your church's effectiveness increase as the Spirit works miracles and healings within your congregation. The list goes on and on.

But before we get too carried away, we need to be honest with ourselves regarding why the bias against being filled with the Holy Spirit exists. Does the Spirit really cause us to be strange and impractical, or do *we* cause these things? Is there truth to the idea that charismatic believers are emotional and without practical wisdom, common sense, and tact? If such extremism does in fact exist, I have to believe that the doctrine of the Holy Spirit is not to blame. I believe that these are learned behaviors, resulting from a lack of discipleship or ineffective leadership by various spiritual leaders and/or mentors. Remember, the shepherds are the ones who should be tending the flock. If the sheep are running wild, are ignorant, or are misbehaving, the leadership is responsible. Our Spirit-filled churches are diminishing due to what I believe is a gross lack of knowledge regarding the person and function of the Holy Spirit in both our world and our churches.

To begin the necessary change, we need to untie the knots between the Bible and tradition, but we must also remember that as believers, we need to be willing to do whatever the Bible truly tells us to do. Just because something has always been done a certain way does not mean that something is biblically accurate. Biblical principle exists for a reason. Once we know in our hearts what is biblical, what is *truly* from God, we can forevermore have confidence in those things. Trust is the key issue here. I heard a preacher once say, "Faith begins where the will of God is known." Once we really know what God's will is regarding a matter, that matter is settled. Further discussion is no longer necessary. It is now a matter of action and/or response. If God wills it, then it must be present in His churches and in the lives of His children.

After all, the Church doesn't belong to us. It doesn't belong to church leaders or church members; it belongs to Jesus. And since God is omniscient, He has known since the beginning of time what would be considered acceptable and what would be considered odd in our generation. In the end, He still filled the Church with His Spirit, and for us to accept the belief that this generation—that the Western church—is too advanced or skeptical to operate like the churches in the book of Acts, then we are questioning the judgment of God Himself.

It all comes down to trust. Do we trust God? Do we trust that the baptism of the Holy Spirit is as necessary as He says in His Word? Do we trust that God's ways are higher and more effective than our own ways? Can He do beyond what we can ask, think, or imagine? In my opinion, it is better to put my trust in God and in His Word than to put my trust in the traditions men have created.

Ephesians 5:18 (NASB) reveals a command to **"Be filled with the Holy Spirit**."In addition, 1 Corinthians 12:31 (NASB) declares, "Therefore, my brethren, desire earnestly to prophesy, and do not forbid to speak in tongues."

Notice that Paul encourages the people of the Church to go after spiritual powers and abilities. He even warns against forbidding the Church to speak in tongues. In other words, we should allow the expressions of the Spirit. In fact, not only should we allow tongues and other gifts, but we also should not *hide* them.

We must remember that Jesus and the Holy Spirit are one. This is *His* church, and He said, "I will build my church and the gates of hell will not prevail against it" (Matthew 16:18). If Jesus wants spiritual gifts, tongues, and the moving of His Spirit in the Church, and if He feels this is the best way to make it effective against its adversaries, then His wisdom supersedes our opinions. It always has, and it always will. Though we may be creative and utilize helpful marketing and branding strategies, we cannot forget that the Church is not our house. As I've mentioned before, the Church is *His*, and there are limits to the methods we should use. So before we cut things out of our belief systems, we must ask the owner of the Church.

> *When I turned to see who was speaking to me, I saw seven gold lamp stands. **And standing in the middle of the lamp stands was someone like the Son of Man**. He was wearing a long robe with a gold sash across his chest. His head and his hair were white like wool, as white as snow. And his eyes were like flames of fire. His feet were like polished bronze refined in a furnace, and his voice thundered like mighty ocean waves. He held seven stars in his right hand, and a sharp two-edged sword came from his mouth. And his face was like the sun in all its brilliance.*
>
> *When I saw him, I fell at his feet as if I were dead. But he laid his right hand on me and said, "Don't be afraid! I am the First and the Last. I am the living one. I died, but look—I am alive forever and ever! And I hold the keys of death and the grave. Write down what you have seen—both the things that are now happening and the things that will happen. This is the meaning of the mystery of **the seven stars you saw in my right hand and the seven gold lamp stands: The seven stars are the angels [messengers] of the seven churches, and the seven lamp stands are the seven churches**.*
> **Revelation 1:12-19, NLT** *(emphasis mine)*

In these verses, the Son of Man is Jesus—the resurrected

King. He's not represented here as a gentle lamb; He's represented in all of His authority and glory. And in His authority and glory, He is walking among the lamp stands, which are His churches. In fact, the churches represented by these lamp stands were some of the most influential churches at the time this book was written.

We also see the stars in Jesus' right hand. These stars represent the pastors of the seven churches/lamp stands. The fact that these pastors are described as "in His hand" reveals that Jesus is very involved in the activities of His churches. The leaders in His hand are not above His authority; they are in His hand for His use, His plans, and His purposes.

Some of the later passages in Revelation deal with Jesus praising or aligning His churches. Some of the churches mentioned even try to treat Jesus like an outsider. In Laodicea, for example, Jesus states He is standing outside of the door, knocking and asking for permission to enter. But even in such an environment, notice the attention Jesus pays to His Church. He isn't indifferent to what we decide—the Church still represents Him and is meant to accomplish His assignments on the earth.

Can we not see that His ideal for the Church is to build a healthy and successful Church? We must be careful not to let our personal bias or inherited belief systems cloud our judgment. We must learn to decipher the truth because it is our embrace of the truth that will equip us for destiny. In the end, it's about trusting the Lord and trusting His Word.

3

Uniquely You

There has been a plethora of opinions and misunderstandings within the Church world, along with a decisive lack of agreement. While agreement concerning every single stylistic element, personal experience, or tradition relating to church life is next to impossible, agreement concerning biblical mandates and doctrines is imperative. Of course, biases and/or disagreements don't always form from malicious intent; they can often spring from over-enthusiastic believers who are trying to do a good thing. Nevertheless, biases can cause irreconcilable rifts, no matter how good the intentions of those involved.

Let me present a practical example. Some Spirit-filled ministers have mistakenly assumed that each person's encounter with the Holy Spirit must be in a manner similar to their own personal encounters. If a person (we'll call him Joe) met the Holy Spirit in a good, old fashioned revival meeting, he might afterwards believe that a real filling of the Holy Spirit can only occur in good, old-fashioned revival meetings. If Sally, on the other hand, fell to the ground underneath a weighty presence of the Spirit, she might think that an experience such as hers trumps other less dramatic encounters. In such a case, Joe and Sally could end up spending a precious amount of time trying to recreate their first encounters, rather than enjoying daily encounters with the Holy Spirit.

I hope you don't misunderstand me here. I do believe in overwhelming encounters with the presence of God during church services or ministry times, but I also believe that we've had the tendency to limit the move of God to the walls of the church. The power of the Spirit is truly meant for ministry and encounters *outside* the walls of the church, and the filling of the Spirit is meant to make this world a better place. In other words, the movement of God's Spirit is about results, increase, profitability in life; it's not only about experiences.

*There are diversities of gifts, but the same Spirit. There are differences of ministries, but the same Lord. And there are diversities of activities, but it is the same God who works all in all. But **the manifestation of the***

Spirit is given to each one for the profit of all.
1 Corinthians 12:4-7 (emphasis mine)

I would also like to issue this warning to my fellow church leaders: you will never be able to please everyone. To some, you will be too extreme, and to others, you might not be extreme enough. For some churchgoers, one extra song in the worship set will cause a shock wave. For others, a service without the interpretation of tongues or three hours of worship isn't truly Spirit-filled. Again, you cannot please everyone, and in reality, you shouldn't try to do so. Pleasing God is your ambition; He knows who you are and whom you were designed to reach.

Does this mean that God will never ask you to do something outside of your comfort zone?

God will always challenge and stretch you. He might even ask you to do things that don't make sense, but He knows what He's doing. Of course, you don't have to create or cause these moments of growth. It's not your job to prove you're Spirit-filled, and in fact, a lot of chaos comes from those who have tried to move God when He wasn't asking them to step out. It's His Church, and your job includes trusting Him and following His lead.

For all who are led by the Spirit of God are children of God.
Romans 8:14, NLT

I like to tell our church that we are children of God, and as such, we should be good at following His Spirit. As a leader, I want to be good at following my God's leading. After all, what He has in mind for today's service is good, healthy, and eternally important.

Why am I emphasizing following His lead so much? It's simple. I want you to realize that you don't have to perform to be Spirit-filled; you don't have to prove your "Holy Ghost-ness." You are to be led by the God who made you and who assigned you to your position. God is more eager than you to reach the people of His Church. He loves them more than you could ever imagine, and He called *you* to lead them. Therefore, you must remember that you are unlike any other person and are not to imitate another's calling or expressions of spiritual activity. You are to be led personally by the Holy Spirit.

It's true that every pastor and church has the same mandate: to seek and save the lost, to destroy the works of the devil, to make disciples, etc. However, every pastor and church also has a different flow (culture and personality) and has a different way of accomplishing that mandate.

In other words, we must be careful to not become spiritually snobbish, thinking our's is the only way.

God can move in an hour, just as He can move in three hours. The Holy Spirit doesn't mind preparedness or pre-planning. He can use pastors in jeans and T-shirts, and not every service has to include the manifestation of a glory cloud.

But, God does desire His people to be more than mere "drop in, drop-out Christians," and there are times in which it is wise to take additional service time. The real issue isn't convenience; it's effective ministry from God to His people. We must remember that the Church is the House of God, the place where people meet God and meet with God. It is both evangelistic and developmental. We not only provide an opportunity for people to hear about God, but we also provide a place where people can actually encounter Him and grow in their relationships with Him. While we must be sensitive to the needs of our people, as well as to the guests who come through our doors, we must be equally sensitive to the plans of God's Spirit for that day.

Sometimes, a Holy Spirit interruption is part of your growth, as well as the growth of your people. Perhaps God's Spirit is stretching both you and them. You may have to step out in faith, while the congregation may have to set aside their preconceived ideas about how a service should go. But let me encourage you. Whenever the Lord has interrupted the plan at our church, not one person has ever been upset by the extra time required.

I remember a recent service when the Lord prompted

me to change things up a bit. All morning long, I heard the word "diabetes" in my spirit. So during worship, I stepped up to the stage and asked those who were battling diabetes to come forward. Approximately eight people came to the front. I then asked the church to stretch out their hands to pray while I gently placed a little oil on the foreheads of those at the front and prayed for their healings. There were no fireworks, and there was no big hype. I just stepped out in faith and obedience.

A few days later, I began receiving testimonies. One man in particular had battled diabetes for over twelve years and was forced to inject himself four times a day with insulin. Over the past seven years, he had even begun to lose feeling in his legs due to neuropathy from the diabetes. That day at church, the Lord restored feeling in his legs, and over the next week, he began to need less and less insulin. As of today, he no longer needs insulin, and he is now able to eat some of the foods previously off-limits to him.

In another service, I felt we needed to pause worship and pray for the sick. However, I first explained to the congregation that it was scriptural. I then told them what I was going to do, which consisted of praying a short prayer, touching the foreheads of those at the altar, and saying, "in Jesus' name, be healed". That's all. Nothing weird. Nothing conjured up. I believe that explaining to people what is about to happen helps them prepare for ministry. Don't assume everyone understands the plan. Walking them through it helps them get their heart ready and keeps things moving efficiently in the service. My verbal directions even help our ushers prepare for what's about to happen, and they can serve the people better as they come forward.

About 100 people came forward for prayer that day. I quickly went down the line and prayed for each of them. There was no yelling and no shaking, and at the end of the day, the interruption only added an additional twenty minutes to the service.

Then after service, a couple approached me. They were missionaries to Honduras, but the woman had been suffering with tremendous back pain. Her doctors and chiropractors were unable to help, and the pain was so severe that the couple was considering canceling their upcoming trip to Honduras. But the Lord totally healed her and removed all of her pain at the altar. Their trip to Honduras was able to move forward as scheduled! Amen!

Each of these testimonies, as well as many more that I don't have space to write about, occurred because the Holy Spirit was afforded the time to touch His people. Praise God for interruptions! And while these interruptions don't occur every week, our church intentionally chooses to provide an environment in which God's Spirit can touch His people.

Let me pause and take a moment to emphasize the word 'intentional'. Each church should keep their unique style—you can be a traditional church, a Word church, a contemporary church, biker church, cowboy church, surfer church, a church that highlights the arts, a hipster church, a *whatever* church, as long as you serve the Lord—but at the same time, each church should also be intentional in making sure the Holy Spirit has room to move when He wants. Again, this is not about you copying someone else's style; this is about prioritizing opportunities for the Lord to move.

Ask yourself the following questions:

"Where is the Holy Spirit in our church culture?"

"Where do people get introduced to the Holy Spirit?"

"Are classes a better place for people to learn about the Holy Spirit than at the altar?"

"How do our children discover the Spirit of God?"

"When can God physically touch His people during our services?"

Unfortunately, many modern churches have devalued the moving of God's Spirit as found in the book of Acts. Remember, our priorities mirror our beliefs. If we neglect to think of the Baptism of the Holy Spirit or of the operation of the gifts of the Spirit as important, we will neglect to provide ample opportunity for them to manifest. So if you want to give the Holy Spirit the opportunity to move, you should provide places for Him in your church calendar, programs, and core values. Provide services where the Holy Spirit is free to move, speak, or touch the people beyond weekly worship and sermons. You could, for example, hold a service once a month or midweek which provides opportunities for Him to move in the lives of His people.

A wise, old preacher once told me something that changed my philosophy forever. He emphasized to me that a problem arises when preachers try to accomplish too much in a single meeting. He told me, "You need to decide the purpose of the meeting and *then* fill the agenda."

Practically speaking, if you're holding a discipleship class, you won't need thirty minutes of worship to get the Spirit moving. Why? It's a class. If your service is about worship, you might not need a sixty-minute sermon attached to the back of worship time. If it's a prayer service, you might not need to teach beforehand. If your priority is to pray for the sick, then don't take five hours singing and talking before praying. Yes, it's good to prepare the hearts of the congregation for what is about to happen, but get to the praying part soon.

In other words, make time management an important part of your service plan. Remember, we minister to *people*, and a human's attention span is only so long.

You're only going to get the best out of them within a relatively short amount of time. I'm not saying you should limit your preaching to ten minutes every week, but I *am* saying that you should take their tired ears and tired bottoms into consideration. They might be coming from a forty to eighty-hour workweek. Even if they are spiritually hungry, and even if their spirits are willing, a long meeting might not accomplish your objective. There is no benefit to wearing people out before getting to the main focus of the evening.

At Life Church, we divide the service into three parts:

1. Encounter in worship
2. Encounter in the Word
3. Encounter at the altar

All in all, our weekend services average ninety minutes. We spend about thirty total minutes in worship, forty-five minutes in the Word, and allow fifteen minutes for the offering, announcements, missions focus, etc. By arranging the service this way, it is our goal to provide an environment for the faithful attendee, as well as the guest, to grow in God. Therefore, worship is not the main event at these weekly services. The teaching of the Word gets more time because it may be the only Bible some people hear all week.

But after the teaching, the altars are open for people to receive prayer. Our altar teams are trained to pray for the sick, to walk people out of spiritual bondage, to pray for the filling of the Holy Spirit, to move prophetically, and to believe God for the impossible. Interestingly, it's common for people to drive one or two hours to our churches just to receive prayer at the end. So even though I may not interrupt a service to move in the gifts of the Spirit, the gifts are mentored into our altar teams and are made available at the end of every main service.

We've structured the service this way because it's my belief that the altar time should be at the conclusion of the service. After I officially end the service and release the congregation, the altars stay open. This way, those who need to leave are able to leave, and those who want to stay do not feel rushed. Even if the altars stay open an additional hour, the entire congregation does not feel pressured to stay and watch.

By the way, it's amazing how many people stay when they have the option to leave. If you give people the permission to leave and then carry on with the service, those who stay will do so because God is moving. Some will, of course, leave, whether it's due to work, baby-sitting, or another reason, and some will continue to watch skeptically. However, many will stay, expecting God to do great things.

We also provide multiple different environments for the people of our church throughout the week and month. We host midweek healing and freedom ministry events, during which we pray for the sick and those bound by spiritual oppression and addiction. We also host midweek classes where we teach people about hearing the voice of God and understanding dreams and visions. For those seeking a biblical education, we offer a Bible school program that meets once a week. We have a midweek prayer service and midweek intercession classes. We also host a monthly Encounter service that is geared toward worship. This is a less-planned service that often changes as the night progresses. There is no way I could accomplish all of this in ninety minutes each week, so we provide other *intentional* environments for the Holy Spirit to work.

Again, I can't emphasize this enough: be intentional about creating environments. You may be a more traditional church leader. Maybe you're more contemporary. Perhaps your congregation is culturally diverse; maybe you only have one flavor of ice cream sitting in your pews. Maybe you reach the hipsters; maybe you reach the business professionals. Whatever your style, your environments can look and sound like you, but you must be strategic as you expose your people to more of God Himself.

Why?

Your people may not otherwise learn how to foster divine fellowship with God on their own. What they learn in church relating to meeting with and listening to the Spirit of God will end up in their personal lives, and they will be grateful for the opportunity to meet the Spirit of God.

My Biggest Stretch Story

Those who know me today may not realize that I wasn't always a "I will lay my hands on you" type of pastor. I've always prioritized meeting God in church, but when we first started, I was predominately a Bible teacher. Our services consisted of worship, teaching, and a response for prayer and salvation. (By the way, the laying on of hands is all very biblical.) I always wanted *others* to pray for people because I never wanted to be put on a pedestal or be the focus of anyone's attention.

But beyond those reasons, I was also afraid of failing. What if nothing happened? What if people came up to the altar and left without a change? I didn't want to look foolish or over-emotional.

Then one day, after a series of meetings with a guest evangelist, I felt that God was planning something different for the upcoming Sunday service. I had tried all week to write a sermon, but nothing was coming to me. Our church was really growing, and there were new families and a great momentum had been building. So I began to panic.

How was I going to stand in front of all those people with nothing to say?

I mean, I could have thrown something together just to fill the time, but I knew God didn't want me to preach. Any preparations I made just felt empty. I knew in my spirit that God wanted me to step out and touch His people.

That morning I can remember trembling during worship, wondering what I was going to say to the crowd. I am not a spooky-spiritual person, and all I kept thinking was, "They're going to think I'm trying to be Benny Hinn or some over-dramatic TV preacher."

Well, worship came to an end, and it was time for me to take the microphone. So I walked slowly up to the stage. I kept my eyes closed and asked the worship team to sing the song again.

Then I asked them to sing it again.

And one more time, please.

After the third time, I had effectively stalled as long as I was able. I was secretly hoping God would do whatever He was going to do without my doing more than standing on stage with my eyes closed. I peeked out of one eye, hoping to see a spontaneous glory cloud manifest, or maybe even a mass revival.

Nothing happened.

All the people were still there, standing on their feet, just staring at me.

So I did what any good man of God would do. I kept my eyes closed and said, "Sing it again."

Finally, a guest to the church, a man who had only attended once or twice, walked from the back of the room to the platform. I noticed him when I tried peeking out of one eye again. I couldn't rightly pretend he wasn't standing there, so I walked over to him and asked how I could help him.

He didn't do anything crazy; he just said softly, "Whatever God has told you to do, do it."

Well, that did it. I couldn't "wait on God" any longer. God was waiting on me.

With my eyes still closed, I told the church that I was going to pray and lay my hands on anyone that wanted me to pray for them. Now keep in mind that I had no specific direction beyond that. I didn't present a call for healing or for the filling of the Spirit. I just knew I needed to lay my hands on those at the front; that was it.

I saw a few people come to the front, and I began my descent from the platform. The time was 10:30 am.

As I laid my hands on the first person, nothing happened. There was no crying or falling down or really any emotional response at all. So I went to the next person. But as I began to move, the Holy Spirit prompted me to return to the first person. I didn't have any words to say or pray, primarily because I didn't know exactly why I was doing what I was doing. Nevertheless, I went back to the first person out of obedience, and as I laid my hands on her again, I felt a remarkable love and compassion fill my heart. God didn't need me to speak; He just wanted my hands so He could touch His people through them.

After that first person, I began to keep my hands on each one until I felt released. With some, I stayed only a few seconds, and with others, I stayed a few minutes. And the whole thing wasn't about *me* at all; God was just loving His kids through a yielding vessel.

As I moved down the line, each person reacted a bit differently. Some of them cried, others laughed, some fell to the ground, some stood worshipping, and some didn't seem moved at all. But after I finished laying my hands on that small line, I looked up and saw that a much larger line had formed and wrapped itself around the room. So I just kept my eyes closed and kept praying that the Holy Spirit would minister to whomever He wanted, however He wanted.

Once I finally reached the end of the line, I opened my eyes, turned to my wife, and said, "Let's go get some lunch."

"Lunch?" She laughed. "You're late for the New Members' class. It's 6:30 pm."

The ministry at the altar that day had lasted eight hours. Can you believe it? Midwest Americans don't stand in line for *anything* for eight hours. Americans want God, but only if they can get Him fast. There's football and food to be considered at all times.

Not this time. Parents put their kids down for a nap on the bleachers in the gym. Some went home, changed their clothes, and came back to get in line for prayer. That day, hundreds refused to be denied the opportunity to experience what God was doing.

That service did something in our church; that day our church became a church that not only talked about being passionate for God, but also demonstrated it. I can't say that we've experienced a move of God quite like that since. God has moved in many different ways, but I believe we made a statement as a church. Collectively, we chose to be open to the Lord, and that same spirit of openness is still present in our church. It can be felt in how the people worship, how they respond to the altar, to offerings, and to outreaches. Our church is better in so many ways because we choose to be open to God and to the prompting of His Spirit.

Chasing Revival

However, an encounter with God can cause hungry Christians to begin chasing after the movements of the Spirit, which isn't, in itself, a bad thing. But it's more important for the people of God to be *led* by the Spirit of God than to chase the movements of His Spirit.

Let me explain what I mean.

Over the years following that service, I definitely

chased after the movement of the Holy Spirit. I chased the ministries where I believed I saw the spiritual gifts in operation. Obviously, there's nothing wrong with spiritual hunger or desiring spiritual gifts (1 Corinthians 14:1). Still, **the key is to pursue *love* and to *desire* spiritual gifts.** Don't chase the gifts. Don't chase the people who move in the gifts. Don't chase the ministries who demonstrate the gifts. Ministries and men can't give you their gifts; spiritual gifts come from *God's* hand. Pursue love. Pursue *God*.

Sometimes, when we see a ministry operating in the spiritual gifts, we overlook their immaturity, carnality, or even spiritual pride. Please remember, it is possible to operate in spiritual gifts while still being carnally minded and spiritually immature.

> *That you are not [consciously] falling behind or lacking in any special spiritual endowment or Christian grace [the reception of which is due to the power of divine grace operating in your souls by the Holy Spirit], while you wait and watch [constantly living in hope] for the coming of our Lord Jesus Christ and [His] being made visible to all.*
> **1 Corinthians 1:7, AMP**

The church in Corinth was spiritually gifted, but they were still considered spiritual babies. Paul devotes whole chapters out of both 1 and 2 Corinthians to teaching the church in Corinth how to operate in their gifts with integrity and humility. He wasn't discouraging their gifts, but he *was* encouraging them to mature spiritually. He challenged them to get along with each other, to walk in sexual purity, and to be selfless at the communion table.

What does all this mean?

It means that a ministry can be powerful, gifted, and even see manifestations of God's Spirit while still falling short in love, character, and self-control.

At first, we allowed people to bring some styles of "moving in the Spirit" into our services without doing our own research on the subject. As a result, we did some things in the name of prophetic movement that may not have accomplished much, apart from making us look a bit odd. I truly believe in modern-day prophets and words of prophecy, but there were a few times when we may have tried to move the prophetic, rather than allowing God's Spirit to move us. I'll explain more about prophetic ministry in a later chapter.

I'm sharing our story so that you can have peace about your own story. Sometimes the pendulum swings too crazy, and sometimes it swings too reserved. But in the end, these experiences helped us to define what we wanted to be and what we didn't want to be.

Balance

Balance is good, but be careful not to equate balance with perfection. You do not have to be perfect in order to move in the Spirit. Many fear offending or confusing someone, or even losing control of the service. But only through practice can we perfect the operation of anything, and avoiding the issue will also not bring balance. If you say, "We believe in the Holy Spirit, but we do not practice the spiritual gifts or manifestations," you are not bringing balance to the situation.

Balance is a process and can only be attained by seeing something in Scripture, obeying it, and practicing it. Finding the extremes and being honest about style and preference are par for the course. But we must also be willing to confront the changeable and the unchangeable when it comes to being Spirit-filled leaders to this and every generation.

But even if you've been burned by the "Charismatic, Pentecostal" movement, please don't let the enemy talk you out of the genuine. There are genuine prophetic movements, genuine deliverances, genuine healings, and genuine miracles that take place in the Church. Please do not neglect these powerful moves of the Spirit or deny your church the experience of the Spirit because of someone else's abuse. If you've seen spiritual abuse, be the one who stands up and changes the standard. The modern Church will never improve if we do not face the issues and intentionally bring the Spirit into this generation with relevance, character, and excellence.

If you're nervous that people can't handle the move of the Spirit, or that the Spirit will drive people away from God, please remember that manifestations of the Spirit are manifestations of God Himself. The Spirit of God is God! It's Him, not another spirit, who will show up in your church. The people, the buildings, and the fruit belong to Him. Of course, you will probably have skeptics and cynics in the pews, but people also often understand and appreciate the gifts of the Spirit more than they will admit. I believe we can all agree that, if the move is of God, it is valuable to both you and your church.

4

What's the Deal with Tongues

Have you ever wondered why God would use a sign like tongues when preparing His plan to fill people with the Holy Spirit?

In this book I've tried to not make the discussion on the Holy Spirit focus on tongues, but I do believe I can add one chapter to this extremely important aspect of a Spirit-filled life or church.

I'm sure some of us have asked the question, "Why tongues?"

"God, didn't you know people would have a hard time with that?"

"Didn't God care that people would make fun of it or even question it's validity?"

Surely God, in His infinite wisdom, would have known that people in our 'sophisticated society' and 'modern age' would be too advanced for some silly gibberish. There must have been a better, more socially acceptable manifestation to go along with the filling of His Spirit.

So why tongues? Why did He choose this controversial manifestation?

First, I would like to help you with the word: *tongues*. Translators used the word *tongues* to describe the unlearned language people were speaking after they encountered the filling of the Spirit. Maybe if the phrase 'tongues' creeps you out or becomes a stumbling block to others, just say 'unlearned language'?

Is it really too hard to believe that the God who made and dispersed languages in Genesis 11 couldn't give you one all of a sudden, as a sign that something has changed within you? On the other hand, what sign would have been more socially acceptable or less awkward? If we are going to criticize the sign He chose surely we would have a better option? Perhaps it would've been less controversial if people lit up and glowed like a light bulb when the Spirit came upon them: would that be less peculiar? In the end, God knows what's best. All of this discussion about the moving of His Spirit in ways He's designed is a trust issue. There is actually a very important reason why God gave you a language to use on a spiritual level.

Language, or the words you say, are very important to God. Look at the following verses:

> *In the beginning was the Word, and the Word was with God, and the Word was God.*
> **John 1:1, KJV**

> *With the fruit of a man's mouth his stomach will be satisfied; He will be satisfied with the product of his lips.*
> **Proverbs 18:20, NASB**

> *Death and life are in the power of the tongue, And those who love it will eat its fruit.*
> **Proverbs 18:21**

> *Truly I tell you, whatever you bind on earth will be bound in heaven, and whatever you loose on earth will be loosed in heaven.*
> **Matthew 18:18, NIV**

The Bible places a huge emphasis on the power of

our words and the ability to speak. Power is released when we open our mouth. Notice in the following scripture that Jeremiah's influence and authority was going to come through his mouth. He would affect nations by the words coming out of his mouth under the power of the Spirit.

> *Then the LORD stretched out His hand and touched my*
> *mouth, and the LORD said to me,*
> *"Behold, I have put My words in your mouth.*
> *"See, I have appointed you this day over the nations and*
> *over the kingdoms,*
> *To pluck up and to break down,*
> *To destroy and to overthrow,*
> *To build and to plant."*
> **Jeremiah 1:9, 10, NASB**

James, in the third chapter of his letter, spends extensive time teaching on the danger of a tongue under the wrong influence. The tongue can destroy your life and others around you. It's by your mouth that you confess Jesus as your Lord. It is through your lips that you can bind the devil and cast him out. Your words will bind up the brokenhearted, set captives free spiritually and emotionally, and release the healing power of God's promises into a person's body. Your mouth and your words are extremely important in regards to spiritual matters. God wants your mouth; the devil also wants your mouth because if he can get you speaking death, fear, unbelief, negativity and the like, he knows you are setting your life and other's lives on course for destruction. When we see the value that God puts on words then speaking with the gift of tongues actually becomes the most valuable asset, in God's mind, that He could have given us. People don't need you to glow like a light bulb—but the words that come out of your mouth, even if you don't understand them, release God's power. Remember, the Sword of the Spirit is the WORD of God. God fights the devil, disease, confusion, ignorance, and sin using words. God creates with words; God heals with words; God blesses with words. You can see that everything God has brought into existence, and into our lives, started with words. Our salvation began by hearing the gospel and confessing Jesus as Lord. 'Tongues' is basically the Spirit of God commandeering your mouth, like a police officer in need of your vehicle to catch a thief on the run. The Holy Spirit needs your mouth!

I am convinced that God continues to need our mouths to accomplish His will on the earth. Yes, He also needs our obedience, but don't forget the importance of your mouth.

In this manner, therefore, pray: Our Father in heaven,

Hallowed be Your name. Your kingdom come. Your will be done on earth as it is in heaven.
Matthew 6:9

In teaching us to pray, Jesus links God's will from heaven with our responsibility to pray that will onto the earth. Prayer is just talking. Prayer is our words declaring God's plan and purpose. Why would Jesus tell us to pray for God's will to happen on earth as God desires it in heaven unless we were genuinely connected to bringing His will through our prayers? If God's will was just going to happen regardless of our prayers then Jesus would not have given us the assignment to pray it into this dimension.

For if I pray in a tongue, my spirit prays, but my mind is unfruitful. What is the outcome then? I will pray with the spirit and I will pray with the mind also; I will sing with the spirit and I will sing with the mind also.
1 Corinthians 14:14-15, NASB

Here Paul distinguishes a difference between praying in your mind (understanding) and in 'tongues', which refers to his spirit praying.

You may ask, "What's the benefit of praying in a language that bypasses your understanding?" I'll list a few benefits and why I believe it's an amazing blessing to be able reach past our limited sphere of knowledge:

- Your words matter to your situation and others.
- God wants your mouth.
- The Holy Spirit will use a language you did not learn to gain the freedom to pray things beyond your understanding.

There are God-sized dreams, plans and strategies that He needs us to pray into our own lives and our world that are bigger than we could ask, think or imagine.

> *For by grace you have been saved through faith; and that not of yourselves, it is the gift of God; not as a result of works, so that no one may boast. For we are His workmanship, created in Christ Jesus for **good works, which God prepared beforehand so that we would walk in them.***
> ***Ephesians 2:8-10, NASB (emphasis mine)***

God has forgiven us and given new life not simply to go to heaven but, according to this previous verse, for good works which God has prepared for us to do. I like to say it like this: God, who thought up the universe with all its wonder and the amazing anatomy of the body which is a miraculous design, has thought up great dreams and good works for your life to accomplish. That's one reason why it's beneficial that God can pray plans into your future that your mind couldn't imagine. As limited, finite beings we often get stuck in where we are in life, rather than where God sees we can go. Our prayers and faith over our lives can be limited by our current realities, good or bad. When we go through low points in our lives it can be tempting to pray small prayers consumed with simply surviving our valley, rather than praying the hope and future God has in mind for us. God sees past our current situations. He knows where we are going and He desires to continue moving our lives in that direction, even though it can be hard for us to see the way through. The darkness of our present situation will pass and we will find ourselves standing strong in the light. So, when we pray in the Spirit with a language that passes our limited understanding, God can keep building His preferred future for us using our prayers. On the opposite side, when we go through very successful times, we can also be tempted to get stuck in our current success. We may think this is the end, that we've arrived in the 'Promised Land', but God knows there are more mountains ahead for you to climb.

Why else would it be beneficial to pray beyond your understanding? Well, if God is praying into my life His will, that I am not currently ready to believe or hear, then praying beyond my understanding keeps me from self-destruction. Perhaps my fear, doubt or unbelief would cut me off from the blessing God is trying to order my steps toward.

Think about the benefit that comes from praying for your children or even your career or business. What about those times when we see problems and we begin praying over the outworking of those problems, even though we don't know the root? For example, praying over our kids' rebellion, where the root of that rebellion is linked to something else that we are unaware of. By praying in the Spirit, God can move into the genuine cause of the rebellion rather then us simply praying out of our own perspective. The same works in our businesses or careers: we may think the problem in the company is Sales but, while praying in the Spirit, God begins to reveal to you that the real problem is in production or in a specific person on the Sales team.

Another benefit I see is in the speed that God can partner with us in praying His will into a situation. Again, my belief scripturally is that God partners with people to accomplish His will. When there is a crisis or a need, God sends a person not an email! God looks for a man or woman to stand in prayer for His will to be manifested in this world.

Let's look at this in the area of an emergency.

Imagine a missionary in danger across the world from where you live. The missionary is being carried to the edge of town to be thrown over a cliff, due to their preaching of the Gospel in the village. God calls people from around the world to get out of bed in the middle of the night to pray. You are on the other side of the world. You sense God calling you with an urgency to pray. You don't have the details—all you know is PRAY! You begin to ask all kinds of questions: "Who am I praying for?", "What's their name?", "What's the situation?", "Is there a family connected to this person?" By the time we ask all our questions the missionary could be already over the cliff. Obviously, that's not a perfect illustration, but the heart behind it reminds us that too many times we don't know what to pray so we don't pray; or we wait until we get understanding before we pray. Praying in the Spirit allows us to pray before we gain understanding.

> *In the same way the Spirit also helps our weakness; for we do not know how to pray as we should, but the Spirit Himself intercedes for us with groaning's too deep for words;*
> **Romans 8:26, NASB**

There are many other benefits to praying in tongues

beyond your understanding, but one final one I'll mention here is that it is a sign that we all have the same Holy Spirit, therefore the same potential and potency to accomplish God's will in our world.

> *While Peter was still speaking these words, the Holy Spirit fell upon all those who were listening to the message. All the circumcised believers who came with Peter were amazed, because the gift of the Holy Spirit had been poured out on the Gentiles also. For they were hearing them speaking with tongues and exalting God. Then Peter answered, "Surely no one can refuse the water for these to be baptized who have received the Holy Spirit just as we did, can he?" And he ordered them to be baptized in the name of Jesus Christ.*
> ***Acts 10:44-48, NASB***

Jesus told the disciples to wait in Jerusalem until they were filled with power and baptized in the Holy Spirit (Acts 1:1-5). When they were filled they began speaking with these unlearned languages: tongues. That was a sign to them that they had received from the Lord the promise of the Holy Spirit. Peter and the disciples knew Jesus was the one giving them this promise (John 16:5-15), that He was approving of them and now filling them.

In the passage above Peter was in a house belonging

to Gentiles—non-Jews. Up until that point the believers had been mostly Jews. Here the Holy Spirit comes upon the Gentiles, thus qualifying them as accepted on the same level as the Jewish Christians. In sharing the same sign—tongues—Peter, and everyone else, understood that God had not only forgiven and saved the Gentiles but also empowered them with the same Spirit that filled the disciples. Peter recognized that the Apostles' filling was the same as the filling of these Gentiles. When we remember that the filling of the Holy Spirit brings with it the power to accomplish the mission of God in our lives then we can see that every believer filled with the Spirit has the same power to accomplish those good works that God has prepared for them. You have the same power that raised Christ from the dead, the same power that Jesus used to heal the sick and raise the dead, the same power the disciples used in starting the Early Church and stand against persecution. It's all the same Holy Spirit. You are not filled with a lesser spirit, or a lesser ability, than anyone else. You can be confident that you have the ONE and ONLY Holy Spirit, with all of His possibilities to be victorious in your calling and ministry assignment. In sharing the same sign we realize that who we have in us is the same. Our talents, callings and giftings may be different, but the source of our potential is the same. The mission that the Lord has given us all is to go into all the world and make disciples, and He has given all of us the ability to be equipped with nothing less then His own Spirit and power. The sign of tongues gives the believer, as well as those around in leadership, the confidence that they are not alone in their calling, and that they are equipped to do more than what was possible in their own strength. They are every bit as much a world changer and leader as the early apostles, having been given the same sign of filling.

So what's the deal with tongues? I believe tongues is a big deal. The power of an unlearned language is a vital part of being an effective, Spirit-filled church. God doesn't give us useless or irrelevant gifts. He knows what His church needs to be most effective. We keep our trust in the Lord—His ways may not be our ways, but they are the most effective.

5

Unchangeable

"What Mountains Do You Want to Die on?"

Growing up, I had a youth leader that used to ask this question: "What mountains do you want to die on?" His goal was to help us realize that not every battle was worth fighting and that we had the responsibility to determine which battles were worth their cost. In the end, it may be more beneficial to agree to disagree on some issues. Then again, it may be necessary to take an uncompromising position.

Below, I've listed a few issues that pertain to Spirit-filled churches and leaders. These are circumstances, which, I believe, are worth the battle.

1: The Need for All People to Be Filled with God's Spirit and Power

Our need for empowerment is undeniable. We live in a fallen world with corrupt cultures and spiritually bankrupt leaders. There's also an enemy that is very real, and he is bent on stealing, killing, and destroying. Christians need more than kind thoughts and good character; we need God's help. We need His ability because His power reaches beyond our own wit and charisma and into the spirit realm. It is *His* power that can reach into the souls of those we are called to reach.

The key here is to avoid extremes. Unfortunately, people who are passionate about the Holy Spirit and His power can become "power hungry." I've seen it happen. Good people choose to pursue the signs and wonders of the supernatural and spectacular. On the reverse side, however, people can become so leery of the supernatural power of God that they begin to pursue only "natural" solutions.

But the answer is not "one or the other"; the answer is "both, and."

For example, discipleship takes work. Sometimes dysfunction is not only spiritually caused, but it is also humanly caused. While I would love to wave my hand and cast out every dysfunction in the name of Jesus, there may be years of habits and thought patterns through which an individual needs to work after the prayer is prayed. Then again, if a dysfunction is rooted in spiritual bondage, mere discipleship will not completely solve the problem. It is in these situations that the power of the Holy Spirit is needed to set the individual free.

Mark 5:1-5 records the story of a demonized man from Gadarenes who had been possessed by demons for years. The Bible calls these spirits "unclean" spirits, which could imply that the man was inwardly tortured by perversion, lust, or unhealthy sexual addictions. The Bible also says that the man had a *legion* of demons inside of him. History tells us that the Romans occupied Israel during the time of Jesus, and a legion of Roman soldiers could include anywhere from three to six thousand men. In other words, this man could have been possessed by *six thousand* demons.

Think about it.

Maybe a legion of demons doesn't shock you, but I think that even *one* demon would be enough to creep most people out. It's amazing how many demons resided inside of this man, and I think that if we look a little closer, there is something powerful we can learn about human beings from this story. Our capacity for spiritual things is mind-blowing. One man alone was able to contain a legion of demons, and we weren't originally intended to contain demons. Why do we have such capacity? We were created in the image of God and created to contain the presence of the precious Holy

Spirit. This is why we have such an amazing capacity. Isn't that incredible? God Himself can dwell inside of us!

Nevertheless, the point here is that a cute program or discipleship system would not have solved the man's problem. It wouldn't matter if they paired him with an accountability partner or if they tried counseling him. All those things are good and beneficial, but in this case, they would not have cured the root problem. **The demonized man needed the power of God**. He needed the touch of Jesus to set him free.

> *How God **anointed Jesus** of Nazareth **with the Holy Spirit and with power**, who went about doing good and healing all who were oppressed by the devil, for God was with Him.*
> ***Acts 10:38*** *(emphasis mine)*

There's a saying we use in our church: "You cannot disciple a demon, and you can't cast out a human being."

Even when you pray and cast out everything imaginable, the problems still sometimes linger. When this happens, it may be due to the fact that a rebellious or dysfunctional human being remains underneath all of the spiritual bondage. In such cases, the only way for that individual to experience freedom is through the alteration of relationships, environments, or choices. In short, they need to make some changes; they need to get involved in their freedom. The Bible tells us to give "no place to the devil" (Ephesians 4:27, NASB). You cannot blame everything on the devil. But, if a person's bondage is on a spiritual level, they require freedom, not just education and accountability.

Now let's take a look at the Bible's account of the demonized man after Jesus delivered Him:

> *Then they came to Jesus, and saw the one who had been demon-possessed and had the legion, sitting and clothed and in his right mind.*
> **Mark 5:15**

Notice that it wasn't until he was delivered that the demonized man was ready for discipleship. Before his freedom, no amount of teaching or discipleship would have saved him, but after his deliverance from the evil spirits, the man was ready and FREE to receive the truth from Jesus.

My friends, we will always need the power of God. At some point a doctor may give a hopeless prognosis, but with the power of God, we can believe that all things are possible for those who believe (Mark 9:23). Of course, we still need to exercise, eat right, and do what we can to stay fit and healthy, but there are times when wisdom and knowledge run short. It is in these situations that we need the power of God.

We also need God's power to succeed in business,

education, and even relationships. The gifts of the Spirit provide help in the workforce as we seek discernment and wisdom, and they also help us to perceive the truth in relationships and to understand the concepts in textbooks.

But from where does this power come?

It comes in the presence and person of the Holy Spirit. I'm so grateful that the Lord has made His power available to us and that He knows we need His ability to solve the issues of life. It is important that we remember it is *His* power, not our power, which gives us the ability to succeed in this human life. I call that mindset humility. Humility is not saying you are lowly and weak. Humility is always remembering your dependence on Him, and in Him you can do all the things He's called you to do. Confidence of Him in you is not having the opposite to a humble heart.

2: Doctrine

In the previous section, I hoped that you would see the *people's* need for God's power and the moving of His Spirit, but in this section, I'm appealing to your understanding. I hope to reveal to *you* that the filling of the Spirit is a biblical doctrine. It is an unchangeable mandate from the Lord, and as such, it needs to be a priority that is budgeted into your calendar.

In the following verses, we can see that it is God's intention to do more than save people from their sins.

He wants to fill His people with the Holy Spirit and with the gifts and power that come with the filling.

If you love Me, keep My commandments. And I will pray the Father, and He will give you another Helper, that He may abide with you forever—the Spirit of truth, whom the world cannot receive, because it neither sees Him nor knows Him; but you know Him, for He dwells with you and will be in you. I will not leave you orphans; I will come to you.
John 14:15

*Then Peter said to them, "Repent, and let every one of you be baptized in the name of Jesus Christ for the remission of sins; and **you shall receive the gift of the Holy Spirit. For the promise is to you and to your children, and to all who are afar off, as many as the Lord our God will call.**"*
Acts 2:38 *(emphasis mine)*

Now when the apostles who were at Jerusalem heard that Samaria had received the word of God, they sent Peter and John to them, who, when they had come down, prayed for them that they might receive the Holy Spirit. For as yet He had fallen upon none of them. They had only been baptized in the name of the Lord Jesus. Then they laid hands on them, and they received the Holy Spirit.
Acts 8:14-17

And it happened, while Apollos was at Corinth, that
Paul, having passed through the upper regions, came to
Ephesus. And finding some disciples he said to them,
"Did you receive the Holy Spirit when you believed?"
Acts 19:1

We can see in these passages that the apostles were intentional in their quest to see the believers filled with the Holy Spirit. We can also see that the baptism in the Spirit is separate from salvation, which means that the baptism is not automatic. In Acts 8:14-17, there was a gap in time from when the new believers received Jesus and when they received the baptism of the Holy Spirit. After they received Jesus, word traveled back to Jerusalem, and then John and Peter planned a trip to Samaria. It was only after this trip that the new believers received the "Promise of the Father," which is the filling of the Spirit. However, I also want you to note the priority that the apostles placed on the filling of the Spirit. They never assumed the filling of the Spirit came with salvation, and in fact, they had to plan a trip to Samaria to see that these precious people received the baptism of the Holy Spirit.

What do the apostles' actions teach us, the modern church?

Well, their actions do not mean that our quest to share the Gospel should fall to the wayside and that we only focus on the baptism of the Spirit. I love the churches that concentrate on sharing the Gospel, and I can't overestimate the importance of new converts. If the Church isn't seeing new believers enter through the doors, then we're not succeeding in the Great Commission. Still, the Great Commission does not end with the addition of new believers.

In the early church, which is the model for the priorities of all future churches, the believers were all filled with the Holy Spirit and anointed, just like Jesus. Jesus was anointed with the Holy Spirit when He was baptized in the Jordan (Matt. 3:16). The first disciples were filled with the Holy Spirit in the upper room (Acts 1), and all future disciples are to be filled in the same way in order for them to accomplish their calls.

You see, focusing on salvation and forgiveness is only part of the story. Of course, the blood of Jesus never loses its power, and it can save and cleanse even the worst of sinners. We could speak about the blood, grace, and renewal for hours!

But here's what I would like you to consider. I think we can agree that the blood acts like a cleansing agent. Like the greatest detergent in the universe, the blood can take our sins away and make our souls as white as snow. But think for a moment about the purpose of detergent. Why do we wash our hands, our clothes, or our dishes? Is it to see them sparkle as they lie in our closets and cabinets?

Hopefully we clean these things so we can use them. We wash our clothes so that we can wear them. We wash our hands so we can use them, and we wash our dishes so we can fill them. In the same way, we have been washed so we can be filled and used.

In fact, the quality of the washing is often a reflection of the value of the "filling" substance. If you're about to put a $100 dollar beverage into a glass, you're going to make sure the glass is clean, no "ifs," "ands," or "buts." Why? You care about the substance that's about to go inside of it.

If the detergent with which you've been cleansed is the very blood of Jesus, then just how precious is the substance with which you are to be filled? God has cleansed you, not so you can remain empty and sitting in a cupboard, but so that you may be filled to overflowing for the use of the Master.

Remember, I'm not dictating a method or style here. All I'm asking is that you consider the value that God places on the baptism of the Spirit. Sometimes, traditions regarding the filling of the Spirit might not work in your setting. Some churches use small groups; others offer altar calls. Whatever your culture, all I'm suggesting is that you offer God's people God's resources to help them succeed against the enemy. After all, if the filling of the Holy Spirit is something that God wants for His Church, who are we to say otherwise?

Jesus is the head of the Church.

Speaking of Jesus, the Bible makes it clear that the baptism of the Holy Spirit is directly from His hands:

> *Being therefore lifted high by and to the right hand of God, and having received from the Father the promised [blessing which is the] Holy Spirit,* ***He*** *has made this outpouring which you yourselves both see and hear.*
> ***Acts 2:33, AMP*** *(emphasis mine)*

Should we not trust what comes from our Savior's hands? Some people are afraid of this baptism, but we never have to fear the gifts that come from Jesus' hands. The same man who died for you has also provided this baptism for you.

After the outpouring of the Spirit, Peter made the following observations in Acts 2:14-18 *(emphasis mine)*:

> *Men of Judea and all who dwell in Jerusalem, let this be known to you, and heed my words. For these are not drunk, as you suppose, since it is only the third hour of the day. But this is what was spoken by the prophet Joel:*
> *"And it shall come to pass in the last days," says God,*
> ***"That I will pour out of My Spirit*** *on* ***all flesh;***
> *Your* ***sons*** *and your* ***daughters*** *shall prophesy,*
> *Your* ***young*** *men shall see visions,*
> *Your* ***old*** *men shall dream dreams.*

*And on My **menservants** and on My **maidservants***
*I will pour out **My Spirit** in those days;*
And they shall prophesy."

First, notice that the outpouring of the Spirit is an outpouring of *God's* Spirit. We're not talking about an ordinary spooky spirit or a spirit force. Through this outpouring, believers receive God Himself. We can see here that receiving the Spirit is not about receiving power for power's sake; it's about God's desire to fill our lives and express His nature in and through us.

Secondly, notice that the outpouring of the Spirit is for *all* flesh. Nowhere is a time, gender, or status limitation expressed. God knows everyone needs His Spirit, and He has made it available to men and women, young and old. I believe that this passage contains one of the most beautiful declarations of equality and freedom in Scripture. In first century Rome, men typically held the upper hand in society, but God doesn't discriminate. He offers His precious Holy Spirit to the rich, the poor, the young, the old, the male, and the female.

Just consider for a moment what the people of that time period heard that day. Throughout biblical history, God's Spirit had been reserved for a special few: priests, prophets, kings, or judges. His anointing was sacred and rare, and communion with His Spirit was closed off, hidden behind a veil in the Temple.

Normal, everyday people could not access the Spirit of God without consulting a priest or prophet.

Now imagine hearing that the same Spirit that was on Elijah was being offered to EVERYONE. The same Spirit that empowered Samson, Samuel, Deborah, and Daniel—that Spirit—was going to be poured out on common men and women. How awe-inspiring! But this was actually foretold by Moses in Numbers 11:29:

"Then Moses said to him, 'Are you zealous for my sake? Oh, that all the LORD's people were prophets and that the LORD would put His Spirit upon them!'"

After Moses' exclamation, God proceeded to pour His Spirit upon seventy other people so that they could assist Moses in his work. Even a few people who didn't show up to the meeting were filled with the Spirit in their tents. Doesn't this story reveal the eagerness of God? The filling of the Spirit was not to make Moses a superstar; God wanted to multiply His spiritual leaders in the earth. This story was a type and shadow of the future filling of all God's people.

When Jesus died, the veil that separated the people from God's Spirit was ripped from top to bottom (Matthew 27:51). Why is the phrase "top to bottom" significant? Think about it; only God could rip the veil from top to bottom. Therefore, *God* initiated the tearing of the veil.

I always thought that the veil was ripped so that man could have access to God, but the Lord changed my understanding one day. Imagine being a parent who is unable to be close to your children. Imagine being separated by a veil from the children you love in order to protect them. You see, God was more anxious to access us than we were anxious to access Him. When that veil ripped, not only could man boldly go to the throne of grace, but God's Spirit could then also dwell in His children.

What would an Old Testament figure say to us today? We're offered this rare, most sacred, and precious gift of God's Spirit, and we sometimes choose to reject it. The same Spirit that parted the Red Sea, the same Spirit that defeated Goliath, that scattered armies, that prophesied the coming of the Messiah—some of us have turned the gift of that Spirit down. The children of Israel could only watch the power of God and His Spirit from a distance, but *we* are being offered close and personal access. Access to the Spirit of God is the greatest gift anyone could ever receive!

The last point I'd like to make concerning these verses in Acts concerns the phrase "poured out." In the Old Testament, the Spirit would come upon an individual for a moment or for a task, but in the New Testament, the Spirit takes up residency in the lives of believers. In other words, once the Spirit is "poured out," He's there to stay. You will never have to wonder if He's there for you. You will never have to beg Him to come and help you. The Spirit of God Himself resides in you and is your HELPER. Truly, you are the temple of the Holy Spirit because He fills you and then remains a part of your life.

3: Respect and Honor for the Holy Spirit

The Holy Spirit is not just another spirit from God; He is the Spirit of God Himself. In the Bible, we are first introduced to the Holy Spirit on page 1. Within the first two verses of the entire Bible, the Holy Spirit is introduced and is moving over the surface of the waters on this planet. The Holy Spirit is IMPORTANT; He was there at creation.

It's also important that we understand that to refuse the Spirit of God is to refuse God Himself. To deny God the ability to move in His Church is to deny more than a Pentecostal doctrine. Those who refuse to accept His Spirit will have to stand before God one day and explain why they thought His methods were no longer relevant or acceptable, which might be a difficult task. I can't imagine trying to convince God that His gift was too spooky, confusing, or unimportant.

Again, to dishonor the movement of the Spirit is to dishonor God Himself. The Holy Spirit is not a cloud or a mist. He isn't a little dove that makes a great picture on church signs. He is not optional. God knows what He likes in His house, and we lack the ability to say we know better than God in regards to anything, much less church function. The Church is His Church, and He knows what's best for it.

4: Clearly Defined Gifts of the Spirit

*There are diversities of gifts, but the same Spirit. There are differences of ministries, but the same Lord. And there are diversities of activities, but it is the same God who works all in all. But the manifestation of the Spirit is given to each one **for the profit** of all: for to one is given the word of wisdom through the Spirit, to another the word of knowledge through the same Spirit, to another faith by the same Spirit, to another gifts of healings by the same Spirit, to another the working of miracles, to another prophecy, to another discerning of spirits, to another different kinds of tongues, to another the interpretation of tongues. But one and the same Spirit works all these things, distributing to each one individually as He wills.*

1 Corinthians 12:4-11 *(emphasis mine)*

In this short list, Paul mentions miracles, healings, prophecies, tongues, interpretation of tongues, discerning of spirits, faith, words of wisdom, and words of knowledge. These gifts are all things for which I'm willing to "die on the mountain."

Let me explain why.

In the above passage we see that the moving of God's Spirit is "profitable." In other words, this is how the Lord brings increase, breakthrough, and success to His body. Often, modern churches will think that the moving of the Spirit will decrease the effectiveness or profit of the church, but God says the opposite. A genuine moving of the Spirit will only enhance life.

But the key word is "genuine." When people lose trust in the moving of the Spirit or His gifts, it is often the result of forgery. Genuine words of knowledge or wisdom, healings, miracles, faith, or discernment will not cause a lack of trust. It's when people (often well-meaning people) make stuff up or are led by their own impulses that people back away.

In Mark 16, Jesus speaks about how the life of the believer should look:

> *And He said to them, "Go into all the world and preach the gospel to every creature. He who believes and is baptized will be saved; but he who does not believe will be condemned. And **these signs will follow those who believe**: In My name they will cast out demons; they will speak with new tongues; they will take up serpents; and if they drink anything deadly, it will by no means hurt them; they will lay hands on the sick, and they will recover."*
> **Mark 16:15-18** *(emphasis mine)*

The bottom line is that there are many instances in Scripture where the body of Christ is given clear direction as to what belongs in the Church. Healing, prophecy, deliverance, and tongues appear in the New Testament over and over again. We see these signs in the lives of Jesus and His apostles, but we also see them appear in others' lives. We see them in operation even in peripheral characters in Acts, such as Stephen and Philip. These men were not apostles, but they still moved in power. Ananias is another example. He wasn't part of the twelve disciples, and yet God sent him to pray for Paul when he was struck with blindness. God wasn't limiting His Spirit to twelve men; He was pouring out His Spirit among the whole Church!

By the way, I'd like to make it clear that I don't believe "they will take up serpents" in Mark 16 refers to dancing with snakes. I believe "taking up" refers to a form of deliverance and that "serpent" refers to the devil's servants or schemes. There are times that we deal with issues all at once at an altar, but there are other times when, as we're growing, we discover an offense or bondage from years past. Getting rid of these is, in effect, taking up those serpents that have remained hidden throughout the years. But regardless of your view on the matter, don't dance with snakes. It's weird.

In conclusion, I believe the four topics I've listed above are topics on which the Church should agree.

Within these doctrinal precepts, there is, of course, the ability to differ in style. For example, some prophets are loud, some speak gently, and some cry. Some never announce that they're prophets, and some will hand you a business card.

But we must have an honest discussion about what the Bible mandates and what is determined by our unique preferences. Flags, dancing in the Spirit, and the use of banners are preferences; they're not a necessity. I'm not trying to challenge the value of these expressions, because I know that many enjoy using them as part of their worship. However, there are certain things we need to be honest about in regards to their *necessity*. Flags and banners *can* be set aside in the event of confusion, distraction, or chaos. In many cultures, these expressions are embraced and enjoyed, but in others, they become a distraction. While there is no biblical mandate for flags or shofars in the New Testament, there are mandates for tongues, healing, deliverance, and prophecy.

Again, I'm not belittling the use of flags, banners, shofars, or spiritual dancing. I'm merely asking that we, as the Church, keep our priorities in view. What is necessary? What is optional?

It can be dangerous for the body of believers to link the moving of the Spirit to flags and banners. Prophetic symbols are great at teaching us about types and shadows, or in helping us visualize spiritual truths, or even in increasing expectation, but they should not be linked to the moving of the Spirit. The Holy Spirit moves by His own will and by our faith in Him; He isn't moved by external imagery. The Spirit is present within us, and He's ready to move when two or three gather in His name. But we do not need to copy the prophets of Baal in the Old Testament and *strive* with outward expressions to get God to show up and perform. His movement is not based on our performing conjured-up 'prophetic' actions, but rather, on the action of Jesus Christ. This is good news! If you ever need Him while you're without a colored flag, He'll still be there, ready to help you in your time of need.

It is not my purpose to offend anyone. Please hear my heart. There are young generations arising that don't understand some of the images, practices, or traditions that I've mentioned previously. They don't get them. And if we demand that moving in the Holy Spirit means blowing horns, these people will move away from biblically mandated issues, such as tongues, healing, and deliverance, in response to the stylistic preferences linked to them. Why should we throw everything away for a tradition that is not a major theological emphasis in Scripture?

If you are debating whether or not to foster a Spirit-filled church environment, please know that you can and should lead a church with your unique style.

Being Spirit-led cannot be defined by a specific style. If you like loud music, then by all means, play loud music! If you like dramas, skits, and short films, go for it! If flags and banners don't fit into your New York or LA style, that is ok! The important thing is that you keep the unchanging biblical mandates in your church services. You must be yourself, not someone else's version of a Spirit-filled pastor. But, for the sake and profit of the body of Christ, please be a Spirit-filled pastor.

6

Changeable

Unfortunately, many people of God are far too eager to fight over insignificant details. Churches have argued, and even split, over details such as paint color, carpet color, or music. The "Contemporary vs. Traditional Music" debate, for example, has been raging for years, even though the traditional music of today was once considered contemporary. Many of the hymns we sing in traditional services were met with strong opposition when they were first introduced. At what age does music become traditional?

But the issue isn't really the music or the paint colors. Change is a part of life, and change inevitably causes conflict. Sometimes, the members of the congregation can offer much-needed perspective and insight, and other times, it's necessary for church leadership to have the authority to make decisions, even if some people disagree with those decisions. Regardless, there has to be a line drawn between the core, unchangeable doctrines that are proven in Scripture, and the necessary stylistic and cultural adaptations.

For example, churches used to focus most of their energies on ministering to adults, but in the past fifty years, the focus has begun to shift toward the youth and young adults. And in the past twenty-five years, a huge emphasis has been placed on children's ministry. Nowadays, a quality children's ministry is a necessity, and I've met a lot of parents who care more about their child's spiritual development than they care about their own development. Of course, we should never neglect adult ministry, but we still must address the culture's demand for children's ministries.

Recently, our church celebrated ten years of ministry, and about six months ago, the Lord began to speak to me about change. In my mind, our church was relevant and excellent, but I began to feel led to change some things. Some of the changes we made were heartily accepted by the congregation, and other changes were met with criticism. But the primary criticism was the fear that the church would become too "seeker sensitive."

Speaking of which, I'd like to take a moment to dwell on the idea of being too "seeker sensitive." First of all, I don't have an issue with churches that are doing everything they can to reach the lost. However, some people use the phrase "seeker sensitive" as a trump card, as a way of accusing pastors of watering down the gospel. But adding lights and modern music to a church service is not changing the heart of the message or watering it down. McDonald's, for instance, can change its packaging and its logo, but no matter how much they change the packaging, a McDonald's Big Mac is still a McDonald's Big Mac.

Now in the 1970s, pews were often teal and pink with a splash of burgundy. That decade loved crazy colors! Then in the 1980s, fake flowers were all the rage. The more fake foliage on the church stage, the better. And today, understated color schemes are preferred, as is the versatility of chairs, compared to the more traditional pews. But again, changing the paint color does not alter the message; it just makes it easier on the eyes of the congregation.

When the Lord first began to deal with me about change, I was a "suit and tie" preacher. I felt that my suit and tie demonstrated a sense of honor and quality, and I wanted to portray my respect for God and His Church as best as I could. In addition, I was also twenty-seven years old when I started the church. I was young, and I wanted to inspire trust from the congregation. I knew that I would be asking the people of the church to commit, to serve, and to give, and I didn't want to come across as an immature kid. Besides, I'm part Italian, and I felt I looked really good in a suit. I could *rock* a stylish modern suit, and I didn't want to dress more causally just because other pastors my age were dressing casually.

But the Lord kept dealing with me to change to a more casual style, and He didn't let me off the hook. So finally, I agreed to dress casually, albeit nice, but I was nervous. I didn't want to deal with questions or have to deal with those who might be annoyed by my "new look." I felt it would be awkward to tell someone that God told me to dress casually.

Now, however, I can see the wisdom of God in that one simple change. I began to have better conversations with people when I greeted them in the lobby. It was as if they felt more relaxed around me, and right away, any sense of class intimidation was removed. Our church has a great food pantry outreach, and not everyone who attends our church can wear nice suits. So when I began to dress casually, the congregation did the same, and I began to realize that most of my membership didn't really enjoy wearing suits. Then, as they began to dress more relaxed, they began to talk with me and one another more, and a feeling of fellowship grew that had once been missing. In reality, the people in my world don't wear suits very often, and by dressing casually, I was able to look more like my people and less like a stage personality.

I did, of course, have some negative feedback from the change. People asked me if I was becoming "seeker sensitive". My response was, "All we've changed is the packaging. We are still preaching the gospel. We're still baptizing people and laying our hands on the sick. We have not backed off from the biblical points of priority, and we never will."

I also began to realize that the apostles of the early Church didn't wear ornate, priestly gowns; they dressed like the people of their times and cultures. Of course, the High Priest's garment did possess elegant details, but these details were ordained by God and symbolic of His ministry to His people. My suit, on the other hand, wasn't symbolic of anything. A person's honor and respect for the Lord cannot be quantified by suits and ties, primarily because what is and is not respectful can change, depending on the culture or circumstance. How expensive is a "respectful" suit? What if you don't own a suit?

I also realize that this example may not apply to everyone, and that's ok. I'm just expressing a specific example from my own set of circumstances. When we changed the packaging, while also keeping the unchangeables, we were better able to communicate the essence of the unchangeables.

I'd also like to take a moment to talk about

"Guestology." Guestology is a word I found in a book produced by Disney entitled *Be Our Guest*[1]. Disney uses this word as they train their cast (a.k.a. employees) in customer service. The underlying philosophy is that each cast member should work to give every guest the best experience possible. They are trained to ask themselves what a guest would need or want to see, experience, or know while at a Disney park, and it works. If you've ever been to Disney World or Disney Land, you can probably attest that the packaging is incredible; it makes a big impact.

Just as theology is the study of God, so guestology is the study of the guests who come through your doors. Each person has spiritual, relational, and physical needs. Some of the people will know what they need, but others will not know what they need. Some may be questioning if they even need God, or they may be wondering what He has to offer. Your job is to help them realize that they need salvation, the Holy Spirit, the Bible, godly friendships, renewal of the mind, etc. As church leaders, we need to think of *them* and anticipate who they are and what they need.

The same can be said concerning your first-time guests. Your guests don't know your church culture or language, your expectations of them, or your facility. They don't know if you're trustworthy or a phony. If

---

1   *Be Our Guest* (Kinni, Lefkon), published by Disney Editions, 2011

someone is stepping foot into a Spirit-filled church for the first time, they could be entering with fear and trembling. What will they encounter? Will their kids be safe in the nursery? Will the nursery be clean or full of dirty toys? They may have heard stories of inappropriate conduct with children in churches, or maybe they've heard stories of pastors stealing the offering money. We are being negligent if we don't consider their thoughts and feelings; we need to put ourselves in their shoes.

Here again, people often push against becoming "seeker sensitive," but to say we should focus on the Spirit of God while not thinking at all about the desires of the people is inaccurate. Does God care about the needs or desires of His people? Of course! So, we should do the same.

Of course, caring about the wants of the people does not warrant the expulsion of God's desire for each service. We should always ask first, "What does God want to do today?" Then we should ask, "How can we make it easier for people to receive what God wants to do or say today?"

For example, if we know that it's going to be a long service with prayer at the end, we could put together a plan to pray for the parents with young children first. That way, the parents are able to receive prayer and also pick up their kids from service before the little ones get too tired or hungry.

I was once at a revival service where the pastor mocked the parents who refused to come to church because of a lack of a quality children's ministry. This particular pastor made it sound like the parents shouldn't worry about their kids, that the kids could just sleep on a chair if the service lasted until midnight. While I don't deny the need for revival services, I do see a problem with children sleeping on chairs for days at a time. In addition, if a four-year-old gets bored after two hours in a service, the mom will feel bad, and the people around the child will get irritated. Some moms may even end up missing the service all together because they won't get the chance to do much more than care for their children throughout the services. They may feel it would have been better not to attend the service at all.

Practicing guestology, on the other hand, requires thinking ahead. It requires anticipating the needs of the guests. For example, could we provide extended childcare for long services, complete with cots and evening snacks? Could we provide a childcare experience that pours the Word of God into the hearts of our kids, giving them a vision to receive more of God on their level? How can we make it easier for the people to receive what God wants to do or say in each service?

We also should not forget about making the information easily understandable for the people. I'm not a fan of the practice of throwing people into the theological "mix" and hoping that they catch up on biblical history and lingo on their own. Some people may be that disciplined, but many won't bother to try that hard. Don't forget the care that Jesus took in making sure that His messages were understandable. He constantly took spiritual truth and illustrated it with everyday pictures. He chose contemporary illustrations to help the people understand. And look at the emphasis that the Apostle Paul puts on understanding, in addition to operating in, the spiritual gifts.

Paul puts it this way:

*So it is with yourselves; since you **are so eager and ambitious to possess spiritual endowments and manifestations of the [Holy] Spirit, [concentrate on] striving to excel and to abound [in them] in ways that will build up the church.** Therefore, the person who speaks in an [unknown] tongue should pray [for the power] to interpret and explain what he says. For if I pray in an [unknown] tongue, my spirit [by the Holy Spirit within me] prays, but my mind is unproductive [it bears no fruit and helps nobody]. Then what am I to do? **I will pray with my spirit** [by the Holy Spirit that is within me], but **I will also pray [intelligently] with my mind and understanding;** I will sing with my spirit [by the Holy Spirit that is within me], but I will sing*

[intelligently] with my mind and understanding also.
1 Corinthians 14:12-15, AMP *(emphasis mine)*

This passage has often been misused as proof that God doesn't think the gifts are all that important, but in all actuality, this passage beautifully illustrates my point. We should be eager to move in spiritual gifts and abilities, and we should be equally aware of those among us who do not understand these things. The goal is not to throw out the gifts; it is to use the spiritual gifts *while* intentionally explaining these gifts. This way, everyone in the meeting can benefit. If a person understands what is going on, he or she is more likely to be open to receive.

I believe that a huge percentage of our charismatic "weirdness," wasted practices, and confusion would disappear if we were to embrace Paul's words here. We can be spiritual. We can operate in the gifts, but we should also pay attention to the people coming into the meetings. Are they being benefited by the service? If not, how can we help them? In other words, care for the questions of your people.

However, please also keep this in mind: **We should love God and love the people, rather than revivals or gifts.**

Sometimes people fall in love with revivals—with the meetings, the power, and the glory—while forgetting about the people. But are the people growing? Are new people attending church? Are they leaving the services changed? Is there a plan for their discipleship beyond the revival services? We have to remember that the purpose of a revival is to help people. The spiritual gifts are only of value when they are helping people. The same goes for our doctrines; they are only of value when they are being taught intentionally and followed by the people.

Pursue love, and desire spiritual gifts, but especially that you may prophesy.
1 Corinthians 14:1

Of course we *should* desire to see the power of God. We *should* desire to be used by God and to feel something glorious, but we should *not* forget about loving God and loving people.

Below, I've listed a few areas on which we've had to work with our congregation. Rather than allowing fear to keep us from practicing any movement of the Spirit, we worked to teach the people of God about these spiritual practices.

1. The Laying on of Hands

You might think that the laying on of hands would be readily accepted or that it is such a prevalent practice that all your guests will come running to the altar as soon as you mention it. However, the truth is that more and more churches never pray for the people in their services. It's becoming more rare for leaders to lay their hands on the sick for healing or on the youth to receive God's call on their lives. In fact, we have people who drive for hours to our church because they've heard that we pray for the sick. In many denominational churches, people never experience the laying on of hands.

There may be many that are concerned about the person who is laying hands on them. They'd rather avoid an overzealous person who becomes overly excited or seemingly out of control. People trust trustworthy behavior and environments. To combat this preconception, we take great care in raising our altar teams. We require classes and accountability from them, and we continue to train them, even after they're on the team. We have conversations about people's fears in receiving prayer and about how we can alleviate those fears. We teach them people skills, not just prayer skills. We also warn them about pushing people to the ground or getting too outwardly extreme. This way, if someone falls to the ground, it will be due to the hand of God alone.

In addition to training, our altar teams are given badges so that our people know whom the church has approved to minister. There's a sense of trust that people give to someone with a badge. Obviously, anyone can give out badges, but word will get around if your church's altars can be trusted. If your people are getting poor ministry from your altars, the badges will be worthless, but if good ministry is happening, word will travel.

I also encourage people to come to the altars for ministry at the end of each service. I explain what it is that they can receive, and I honor our altar volunteers by building trust in their ministries, publicly affirming them during the altar call. As a result, week after week, the altars are filled with people, and they are being touched by the Holy Spirit.

2. Receiving the Baptism of the Holy Spirit

How did you receive the baptism of the Holy Spirit? What was the environment like? Was that method the best way? Are there other ways? Some of us have stories of tarrying all night to receive the Holy Spirit. Some prayed through the night. Others came to altars surrounded by people shouting in their ears.

Sometimes, environments such as the ones listed above can be stressful and intimidating. Some people won't come to the altar because they are scared of altar ministry. Or, maybe they walk away from the ministry feeling dejected because they don't think they received the Baptism like everyone else.

Can we provide better, less stressful environments? Do we have to yell and sweat to see someone baptized?

Have we done an adequate job of explaining who the Holy Spirit is and what it means to be filled? Have we given them the opportunity to ask questions?

I am aware that in the Bible, the Spirit just fell on the people. No one had classes before they received Him, and I don't believe that people necessarily *need* a class to receive the Holy Spirit. However, in comparison to the early days of the Church, many of our people have been exposed to negative information or experiences. In some churches, for example, it's taught that speaking in tongues comes from the devil. These people may need an explanation or some questions answered before they are willing to receive prayer. On the other hand, some have been taught that the baptism of the Spirit isn't for everyone and have stopped seeking the Spirit as a result. Some have been pushed to the ground with people shouting for hours with no tangible results. I know that may sound extreme, but for those of us who've been in weird services, we've seen it all.

Again, we should be asking ourselves what we can do to help them. We must try to walk in their shoes.

So can we create less stressful environments? Yes, we can. It begins with the setting, the timing, and the style of music (if the situation requires music). There's nothing wrong with loud drums or a passionate prophetic environment, but you should be aware that such a setting can create yelling and a bit of a passionate frenzy. People are going to try to shout and pray over the music. Bringing the volume down may help to put some people at ease. I'm not saying one method is better than another, but I am saying that it is helpful to be mindful of your environment.

Can people receive the baptism of the Holy Spirit in small groups? Absolutely! Can they receive Him in or after a class? Yes! As I mentioned before, you know your culture and the setting of your services. Just make sure that your people have the understanding necessary, and then provide an opportunity to receive Him.

But all things should be done with regard to decency and propriety and in an orderly fashion.
1 Corinthians 14:40

What is decent and orderly for your generation, culture, and setting? Culture will always change over time.

3. Prophetic Words and Tongues and Interpretation

In the passage from 1 Corinthians 14 (mentioned above), Paul was addressing the use of prophecy and tongues in church. The Corinthian church was growing, and more and more people wanted to speak during services. As a result, people were speaking out of turn, and the services were becoming a bit chaotic. In and of itself, a bunch of people who want to say something is not a problem, but as a church grows, certain tendencies have to be addressed in order to keep the service flowing.

What I'm about to share is entirely my opinion and a conclusion I've drawn from trial and error. You don't have to follow the example I've outlined, but I encourage you to seek the "decency and order" that makes sense in your environment. It's essential that we don't confuse people or throw the moving of the Spirit out of our services because we're afraid of the people getting out of hand.

At Life Church, we've developed a school for those who feel called to operate in the prophetic gifts. It is through this school that we get the chance to know them and to test their gifts, as well as their hearts. After all, it is possible to be both gifted and to have a proud heart. Regardless, through this school, we are able to see whether they truly have a heart for the people, or if they only have a heart to showcase their gifts. It is also through this school that people learn to hear how the voice of God sounds to them. They get the chance to minister in the school's classes, and as we build trust, they are able to minister in special altar services or to travel with me or other pastors on staff. This school gives these individuals an environment in which they can learn and grow, and in which they can even miss 'it' at times without feeling bad. In the Bible, the prophet Samuel also developed a school for the prophets, and I believe it is very beneficial to provide such an environment. This way, the congregation isn't treated as guinea pigs.

Some of our churches today have hundreds, if not thousands, of attendees. Can you imagine the chaos if everyone took a turn to prophesy? In addition, a Sunday morning church service of a hundred people is filled with people who are either going to be benefited by an interruption of a prophetic word, or they're going to be turned off by it. I do not allow strangers to walk up to the microphone, take it from my hand, and say whatever they feel the Lord has told him or her to say. But that is exactly how many churches deal with the prophetic and the interpretation of tongues—anyone at anytime is allowed to interrupt the service and say what they want. But what if they miss it? Then I publicly have to tell everyone, "Bless so-and-so's heart, but he's wrong." Or, if they speak heresy, I have to change the direction of the service and teach against that heresy. If they have nothing of value to say, then the congregation is left wondering why we just stopped the service for something so . . . vague.

In our church setting, we encourage our people to write down the words they believe they receive from the Lord, or to share them with their prophetic team leaders.

This way, we can judge it *before* it's brought to the congregation. In a smaller church, it may be possible to know whom you can trust, but in a larger church, it may be more beneficial to find these things out in a class setting, rather than in front of the whole church.

Again, you are free to disagree with our method here. My heart in employing this system isn't to remove tongues and prophecy from our services, but rather to bring clarity, order, and function to our culture and environment. Hiding the gifts of the Spirit is wrong; finding how and where they fit into a service in your culture is our responsibility and privilege.

4. Environments

I know that I already touched on forming environments earlier in the book, but I wanted to take a moment to repeat the discussion here. We often lose the opportunity to minister to new people without realizing the true cause of their failure to return. We might think the devil is to blame, or maybe we think that the anointing was too strong for them. Or, maybe we figure that they are too shallow or carnal to appreciate our powerful church. Honestly, it may have nothing to do with the devil or our anointing; sometimes it's our environments.

Sometimes, it's also the length of our services. I want to make it clear that I don't think long services are always a bad thing, but at the same time, long services are not necessarily more anointed. I've been in services that were long because of poor time management and disorganization, but I've also been in two-hour services that felt like they were five minutes long. When the Spirit of God is moving, two hours can feel like five minutes, but when He's not moving, five minutes can seem like two hours.

Actually, our Sunday services used to average two or two and a half hours in length. Amazingly enough, we still grew in numbers during that time, but today, our Sunday services average ninety minutes in length.

So what changed?

We began to create other environments to facilitate some of the elements we thought we had to accomplish on Sundays. We used to think that Sunday mornings had to include times of extended worship, as well as a less-structured flow to the service. However, we found while some were engaged in that extended worship, others were merely enduring it or not understanding it at all. For the guest from a different church background, standing still and singing unfamiliar songs for an hour was more than they wanted to handle. It was too much too fast, because after the worship, they were expected to listen to an hour-long sermon and then to come to the altar for ministry. While many found the format helpful and encouraging, many also found that the whole thing just took too long.

So we decided to make our Sunday morning services a sampling of the best we have as a church. We decided that a taste of worship was better than overwhelming the congregation. I used to think that I couldn't preach for less than an hour, but now I preach for approximately forty minutes. Yes, I do have to leave out great information, but people are now engaged throughout the entirety of the message. In the past, people's eyes would begin to glaze over after about fifty minutes. In addition, the new time limit helps me get to the point more quickly.

Again, some may think that we're being too "seeker sensitive," but we've not changed one piece of doctrine. Paying attention to the value of our people's time and energy is not against our doctrine. Jesus, for example, not only preached His sermons, but He also watched out for the people's physical needs. He fed thousands of them after they stayed to hear Him preach (Matthew 14:13-21). Jesus was concerned that the people were hungry and tired and that they might faint when they left. Notice that He didn't tell the people to toughen up; He showed them concern and understanding. Yes, people need the spiritual, but they still live in the physical.

You may also find that you want to re-label some of your ministries in order for your congregation to understand them accurately. For example, I believe in deliverance   ministry.   With   all   of   the   hurt, disappointment, addictions, and sin that people experience in this world, I truly believe that people should be shown how to forgive others, themselves, and to come out of agreement with old behavior patterns. I also believe in casting out the spiritual bondages on people's lives. That being said, I don't believe that the word "deliverance" is the best word to use when drawing people to the ministry. You are, of course, allowed to disagree with me, but I believe the word "deliverance" brings horror movies to mind. With all the Hollywood drama, saying the word "deliverance" could cause people to envision all types of strange phenomena, such as rolling around on the floor or screaming. This is why we call our deliverance ministry "Freedom Ministry." It explains to the average person the purpose of the ministry, while also allowing them to view the experience with less bias. The word "deliverance" is not sacred to me, but the ministry operation, on the other hand, is sacred.

We use the same philosophy when we talk about our prophetic ministry. We don't call our leaders "prophets," and our prophetic class is called *Hearing the Voice of God*. Why? The title "Pastor" is more accepted and comfortable to the people in the area. No, there is nothing wrong with the title of "prophet," but prophets in my area don't have the best reputation. When people hear "prophet," they also hear "showman." We want the people to receive the ministry of the Spirit, and anything we can do to remove barriers, confusion, and bias is worth it.

In other words, the local church should exercise guestology. I've only listed a few examples above, and there are too many areas for me to cover in this book. However, let me reiterate that you should never feel that you have to compromise your true beliefs to make people happy. People are most happy, whether they realize it or not, when they are in an environment in which God is allowed to move. The key is to keep the goal of connecting people to God in the forefront. If someone is missing out on an aspect of ministry, we must ask why and how we can change. The changeables are the things that function as roadblocks of confusion, frustration, or ignorance.

6

Planning Vs. Spontaneity

My wife and I have four children. In other words, we live very busy lives. I bring this up because one of the most difficult things for us to do is to plan dinners ahead of time. Picking the menu can be a constant point of frustration during busy seasons.

What should we eat this week?

What are the kids bored with?

What's healthy? What's easy? What can we feasibly pull off with this week's schedule?

Normally, when we fail to plan that week's meals, we end up with fast food, pizza, or pancakes. All of these things are edible and easy, but they're not very healthy.

Very little thought went into the planning, and so, little value was reaped from it.

Why do I bring this up?

When we plan our sermon series, classes, outreaches, and environments, we can make sure that our Spirit-filled churches are receiving balanced "diets," and we can be intentional about the spiritual food they're receiving. Too often, Spirit-filled leaders plan week-to-week without an eye on the big picture. Where are you leading the people? How will you judge a successful year? Do you base success only on numbers? How will you know that you have fed the sheep well, challenged them effectively, and given them the opportunity to grow?

Yes, the Holy Spirit can give us the words to speak when we are spontaneously called to preach, but I do not believe that this is the way we are meant to run a church. A sermon series, for example, can help your congregation really understand a specific concept. You can share on it for a month, give or take, and this way, the people are not getting fifty-two unconnected messages. They can hear and digest twelve developed thoughts or ideas.

Planning can also help with creativity. For instance, if you know about an upcoming sermon series, you can begin to see things around you that you can use to illustrate your point. Then, you can place life examples in your messages. In addition, you can promote your sermon series to your people, and you can have them invite their friends.

We've all probably heard the phrase, "If you fail to plan, then you can plan to fail." The value of planning is obvious. It can also keep us from the Saturday panic. You know what I'm talking about—it's the "What am I going to say tomorrow?" panic.

But doesn't planning quench the Spirit?

No, it doesn't. However, if the Spirit moves in another direction that weekend, the plan can go away. I've trained my team this way because it's His Church, not mine. Nevertheless, we can still show up with a plan. God is a God of order, not disorder. Even the Bible constantly illustrates this concept.

For example, when God started creation, the earth was formless and void. He brought it into order and then filled the earth with His creation (Genesis 1). The tabernacle is another great example. God gave Moses a very specific plan, with detailed patterns, and it wasn't until after Moses fulfilled the *plan*, that God filled the tabernacle with His glory (Exodus 25-27). The human body is another great example of incredible design and order. The Lord pours our new human spirit into a body that He ordered and designed.

Throughout Scripture, there are many more examples of structure preceding the miraculous. Even the Church is a great example. God created the Church, ordered it with Christ as the head, and then filled us with His Spirit. And when the churches were operating out of order, Paul was inspired by the Holy Spirit to re-educate them so that the Spirit would be able to move more effectively.

Design is not a hindrance to the Spirit. Think about it. When something is out of order, such as a vending machine, it doesn't work properly. But once the order is set right, things work. Of course, we must be careful to ask God's direction in making plans. We shouldn't make plans and *then* ask God to bless them. Still, we should keep in mind that the Lord made plans, even at the beginning of creation, and so His blessing has been on planning from the beginning.

7

Teams

And he gave some, apostles; and some, prophets; and some, evangelists; and some, pastors and teachers. For the perfecting of the saints, for the work of the ministry, for the edifying of the body of Christ:
Ephesians 4:11-12, KJV

When I was young, I looked up to the pastors in my life. They were like superheroes to me. While other kids idolized sports stars and rock musicians, I admired pastors and other people who I categorized as world changers. They seemed to have the whole Bible and all the questions of life figured out. Now, while I am grateful for the leaders I've been privileged to know, I have come to realize that they are all human. Every single anointed preacher, healing evangelist, prophet, and skilled leader has been and is a normal human being.

I've also come to understand that we've created a divide in our minds between the "ministers" and the "normal people." Unfortunately, some ministers have erred by building themselves up and hiding behind their stage personalities, but in the end, we all need each other. We are all called to the same mandate, and each part of the body of Christ is equally important. Every member of the body of Christ is no less than a part of the image of Christ.

In Ephesians 4:11-12, we can see the design for the early Church. It was not composed of a few "special ones" called to minister while everyone else paid the bills. Instead, the five-fold ministry offices were given to the body of Christ to benefit the whole.

> *Wherefore he says, when he ascended up on high, he led captivity captive,* **and gave gifts unto men.** *(Now that he ascended, what is it but that he also descended first into the lower parts of the earth? He that descended is the same also that ascended up far above all heavens, that he might fill all things.) And* **he gave some, apostles; and some, prophets; and some, evangelists; and some, pastors and teachers; for the quipping of the saints for the work of ministry.**
> **Ephesians 4:8-12** *(emphasis mine)*

From the verses above, we can see that the gifts given by Christ were given in order to equip and perfect the body of Christ. In other words, these gifts were given to help the body of Christ win!

Think about the nature of a gift for a moment. Which is more important in the grand scheme: the gift or the receiver? Imagine God as the giver. Is the giver more excited about the gift or about the receiver's reaction to the gift? If God were to send His ministry gifts via UPS, would He be more excited about the UPS truck and its boxes? Or, would He be more excited about the children that were going to receive His gifts?

Remember, God's focus is His children. These gifts are given to benefit His Church and to help them win in life. If someone is given the opportunity to minister in a gift, the purpose is to benefit the body of Christ as a whole.

In the Old Testament, the phrase "man of God" is used often to represent the prophets or spiritual leaders anointed by God for specific purposes. When I was a kid, most of my Sunday school lessons revolved around one or two key Old Testament heroes, and the intent was to inspire the emulation of their strengths or right choices. I learned about Moses, Samuel, Deborah, and Elijah, and I left intent on becoming a "man of God."

While there is nothing wrong with learning from

Bible heroes, a problem arises with the mentality that God is still only choosing a limited number of people to do His work. Even in today's churches, people have the tendency to get too focused on the "man of God" and his actions, rather than on their own responsibilities and capabilities. But in the New Testament, God set the standard by pouring out His Spirit upon *all* flesh. In other words, young, old, male, female, slave, and free are *all* able to be filled with the same Holy Spirit that was on these great biblical heroes. Every member of the body of Christ has the ability to use the name of Jesus with His authority. In the eyes of the devil, *every* believer is a threat.

> *And hath put all things under his feet, and gave him to be the head over all things to the church, which is his body, the fullness of him that fills all in all.*
> **Ephesians 1:22-23, KJV**

I realize that some pastors may want to feel special and set apart, but in Christ, everyone is special and set apart. As ministers, our responsibility is not to tell everyone about our value, but rather to help the rest of the body realize their value in Christ. As ministers, we must work to mobilize the saints for the work of the ministry. Helping the body of Christ walk in her destiny is the only way that our global assignment will be accomplished.

However, the only way to begin mobilizing the body of Christ is to make team-ideology a part of our culture. Our churches should not revolve around a one-man show, but they should be representative of a body filled with God's Spirit. We should establish a team mentality among our staff members and even amidst our volunteers. Simply put, the more teams we establish, the more players we will have on the field.

Of course, building a team takes intentionality, quality control, trust, patience, relationship building, and much more. Effective team members require training and experience; they need opportunities to try and fail. In addition, spiritual leaders need to learn to be relational, and, even though they may demonstrate a dynamic spiritual gifting, they should not let it overshadow the building of relationships. Jesus, for example, was more spiritually gifted than anyone, but He was able to build relationships. He ate with His team, spent time with them, and mentored them. Notice how He didn't hide in solitude for fear that the people would become too familiar with His anointing. The gift of a spiritual leader can become a great weakness if care is not taken to keep perspective on the lives of the people you have been gifted to serve. Success in ministry is not measured by how much ministry the few can accomplish in front of the many; it's measured by how many can be equipped to minister alongside the few.

If you're wondering what types of teams should become a part of your church culture, remember that the Holy Spirit places the members in the body. He gives talents and ideas to certain people according to His purposes. Look around your congregation, there may be the ability to form prophetic teams, healing teams, freedom (deliverance) teams, evangelistic teams, church planting teams, missions and outreach teams, creative arts teams, etc. Each team, whether listed here or not, needs good people who are filled with the Holy Spirit. We must help all of our people to see the value in their gifts and talents, while also helping them find their place in ministry.

For example, one of the greatest joys I have is sitting on the platform, watching volunteers lay hands on people. I know these leaders are well trained, committed, and trustworthy with the information they hear at the altar and how they will treat the people that come. They can also take more time with people at the altars than I ever could. I am normally only able to touch each person briefly, but the team members are able to ask questions, deal with a person's unforgiveness, and lead people in repentance. It's when these teams minister that we see such great results.

Teams also provide a great opportunity for traveling. When I travel, I am able to bring a team or two with me, and I've observed that those who travel with me return feeling valued and refreshed. It's such a great opportunity to give the people on your ministry teams the chance to see new places and to minister to new people. They can come back to the church feeling like they are living the book of Acts; it makes the Bible real and relevant to them.

Take a look at the upcoming generation. They are determined to have a voice. They use Facebook, Twitter, and all sorts of social media to express themselves. In other words, they want to participate in what is being discussed. They are no longer satisfied with hearing about your anointing or reading about the miracles of the past. They want in; they want to participate. In order to be relevant, we must get people involved in the operation of the gifts of the Spirit.

To accomplish this task, I teach my people that the stage of the church is too small for the gifts that God has placed within them. So many Christians are looking for a platform to validate them, but that mentality is a result of the "man of God" superiority complex we've created in our churches. Each and every member of the body of Christ was on God's mind when He gave the gifts to the Church. He gave them the gifts to help them, to train them, and to enable them to win. That's why pastors have a stage, to help our people realize their ministries in the earth.

In other words, we must build teams in our churches.

We need to find a way to train our people to move in dreams, visions, healings, prophecies, intercession, and miracles in the local church, everyday life, and around the world. The point is to help our people discover their giftings, train them in ministry, and send them out into the world.

8

The Willingness to Confront

How is it then, brethren? When ye come together, every one of you hath a psalm, hath a doctrine, hath a tongue, hath a revelation, hath an interpretation. Let all things be done unto edifying.
1 Corinthians 14:26, KJV

For God is not the author of confusion, but of peace, as in all churches of the saints.
1 Corinthians 14:33, KJV

In these passages, the Apostle Paul discusses how to address things that are done in the name of the Holy Spirit. Apparently, the Corinthian church was experiencing some confusion, or at the very least, some disorderly meetings. Everyone was sharing "a word," a prophecy, or a "tongue." Maybe people weren't really listening to the Spirit, or maybe they didn't realize that they needed to wait to share what they had heard from the Spirit. Regardless, the bottom line is that if Paul had to train people in appropriate spiritual behavior and conduct, you'll have to do the same. You'll need to show people how to use their gifts for good and not harm. You may even need to tell them, "That's not biblical", or, "That's not tactful." Whatever the case may be.

There are some churches, for example, that have been conditioned to allow anything so as not to "grieve" the Holy Spirit. As a result, during the second song of slow worship, Grandma Bertha always gives a tongue, followed by a long silence while the pastor sweats it out, hoping someone will interpret the tongue she gave. Sometimes, Bertha may even interrupt the sermon to give a word. Then, the pastor is forced to disregard the message he prepared and switch topics.

In sticking with this method, you may be keeping Bertha happy, but droves of people may also be leaving the church. Why? They're not learning anything! Or, they're seeing the confusion, disorder, and the lack of value in these interruptions. While you may have grown accustomed to the chaos, the visitors see what you're missing.

I believe we may grieve God more through the disorder we allow than by training our people to work together with clarity, meaning, and value. When people operate in immaturity or a lack of knowledge in regards to the Spirit, other people have the tendency to leave. When "Spirit-filled" is demonstrated as "chaotic, flaky, supernatural weirdness", the people who come to your church might prefer to stay free from the so-called "Spirit-filled" crowd.

Don't get me wrong. I don't blame Bertha; I blame the pastors. She's probably just doing what someone else once modeled for her. Maybe it's a generational dysfunction that no one bothered to correct. It's our responsibility to be overseers, which means it's our job to teach the people proper decorum.

I've had people come in and Karate chop and war dance during one of our worship services. It's my assignment to ask them why they did those things. They told me that they were warding off the devil . . . or something to that effect. At that point we are to teach them that Jesus has already defeated the devil and that if Jesus' blood didn't ward off the devil, their karate moves certainly weren't going to do so. Our faith is in the finished work of Christ, and we enforce that with our prayers, worship, and words. If we want to see the devil run we say, "It is written," not "Hi-yah!"

Another situation arose after certain revival meetings. Members of the congregation wanted to "shake" whenever they prayed or felt the Spirit moving. Perhaps their original experiences were very real, but that does not mean that shaking was meant to be a trademark of the Holy Spirit. In other situations, people would fall down, no matter who was praying or what was being said. They were falling because they believed that it was a necessary action in order to receive from the Holy Spirit. But again, falling down is not a prerequisite for an experience of the Spirit.

As spiritual leaders, it's our job to lead these people in their spiritual development. We need to help them process their encounters with the Holy Spirit and to help them see that the Lord can move in many different ways. There is no need to be determined to experience only one particular expression of the Spirit. In addition, we also need to stress the more prevalent biblical manifestations that are for the profit of all (1 Corinthians 12:7). While the manifestations of falling down or shaking might have profited the individual during a genuine experience of the Spirit, many manifestations of the Spirit move us to help someone else.

Of course, this doesn't mean that we should become

judgmental of everything with which we're not comfortable; God will often move in ways outside of our personal comfort zones. He can also do things that overwhelm our normal, emotional responses. But we should keep moving forward, while also choosing not to worship any one response we had in the past to the Spirit. If we create traditions that demand a certain reaction to the Spirit, we could end up missing a new or present move of the Spirit.

Teaching your people the truth about the Holy Spirit can also help keep the atmosphere in your church safe, fresh, and real. If your people are taught the Word, they will also be able to teach others the truth about the movement and expressions of the Spirit. Priscilla and Aquilla present a great example of this concept. In Acts 18, these two people came across a faithful and passionate man named Apollos. However, while Apollos was very passionate, he only had half the story. He had only heard of John's baptism and had not heard the way of the Lord regarding Christ. But when Priscilla and Aquilla explained the revelation of Christ, Apollos made the adjustment in his preaching and became one of the most prominent preachers of the early Church. In fact, the church at Corinth even wanted to name him their father of faith.

Regardless, the point here is that Priscilla and Aquilla did not have to send Apollos to Paul for explanation, nor did they write him off as an ignorant fraud. They respected his journey and helped him as he pursued his calling. Then, with a few adjustments, Apollos became a skilled minister of the gospel.

Regarding the members of our congregations, Paul teaches in 1 Corinthians 14 that the spirit of the prophet is subject to the prophet. In other words, the believer is well able to control the spiritual urges he or she experiences so as to keep order in the service. It's important to realize that this control is not "quenching" the Spirit; it's clarifying it. I believe that a church truly led by the Spirit is not a chaotic mess. A church led by the Spirit of God is life changing.

However, when offering correction, I do my best to correct people in private. In fact, "mentoring" is a better word to use here. Many people have never had any direction or guidance in regards to their movement in the Spirit. I once ministered with a leader that would get so "drunk in the Spirit" that he couldn't control himself. That is, until I showed him the verse in 1 Corinthians 14:32—that the spirit of the prophet was subject to the prophet. This person was seeing great testimonies and witnessing great moves of the Spirit, but he was also unable to reach the people who walked away because of the chaos that ensued when the Spirit "began to move."

Then again, I have also had to stop some prophetic words publicly. Most of the time, I'll have to stop them because of biblical inaccuracy. Often, these dear people will think that they have received revelation or discernment, but the truth is that God will not misquote His own Word. Any prophetic word should line up with God's words in the Bible. Other times, I've had to stop a word, not because of misquotation, but because the word does not edify, exhort, or comfort the Church (1 Corinthians 14:3). In some cases, these "words" make it seem like God hates His Church more than the devil hates it.

Basically, it's important to ask if the word coming forth has any value. If God is truly interrupting a service, then the word should be equivalent to breaking news. I'm talking, "This just in…" type of stuff. At the end of a word that interrupts a service, there should be a point of action or some revelation that the whole congregation needed to hear right at that moment. However, most of the time, we end up hearing, "My people, I love you, and I'm coming soon." Of course, these statements are true and great, but they're not breaking news. A good example can be seen in Acts 11:28, when Agabus stood up and prophesied a famine. After his word, the congregation knew what to do and how to prepare for the upcoming lack of food. If no idle word should come from our mouths (Matthew 12:36), then no idle word will come from His mouth either.

Please understand: it is very important we correct errors. If someone begins speaking out in service, judge the content, the accuracy in comparison to Scripture, and its value in the moment. When people simply quote a Bible verse with no application, their words can cause confusion or can hinder others from valuing the movement of the Spirit. More than likely, the person you need to correct felt something special, got excited, or blurted out the first verse that popped into his or her head.

In other situations, the abuse of spiritual gifts comes from an overemphasis of a particular manifestation. Just like in any other situation, balance is the key to a healthy spiritual atmosphere. When a person or group of people find out about a spiritual gift for the first time, they may overemphasize that one gift. Whether it be healing, prophecy, or deliverance, a new idea can come across as the answer to every problem or situation. But we have to remember that these "new" ideas are not actually new. They're just new to some people. Also, thinking one gift of the Spirit is the answer to everything is dangerous. Imagine discovering a hammer for the first time and then trying to use it to fix every problem in your house. You'll eventually end up doing damage to your house, even though you're using a good and beneficial tool.

Perhaps it would help to think of the movement of the Spirit like a river. Along this river, there are many streams and brooks, but none of these streams or brooks can claim to be the entirety of the river. Still, every stream and brook is beneficial to the flow of the river. Now imagine that people move along this river and can discover the streams and brooks along their journeys. The problem comes when a person hangs out along only one stream and refuses to move to another stream; each stream and brook should be visited. Abuse and error can happen when someone thinks that their one "stream" holds all the answers or that their "brook" is better than all the other brooks. To clarify, healing, deliverance, and the prophetic are all examples of brooks and streams. In addition, Christian counseling, small group discipleship, evangelism, and financial management can be streams or brooks. But remember, through all of these areas runs the river of the Spirit. He has given us everything we need for life and Godliness, and His flow will often lead us in and out of streams and brooks as He sees fit.

However, please also realize that as you and your team begin moving out in spiritual gifts, you will face disappointment. Prophetic words may fall flat, or perhaps you and your team will pray for the sick with no results. In these moments, don't point fingers or accuse your team of a lack of faith, or even begin accusing the person who died. Just trust God with those mysteries and pray for the next person. Never be afraid to be honest. Never be afraid to address the feelings of disappointment among your congregation. It's ok to admit that you don't have all the answers. There are many things that we don't yet know, but we are accountable to preach and operate in the things that we *do* know. You may not have the answer for why a person in your congregation passed away, but you do know that Jesus commanded believers to lay hands on the sick, to call for the elders of the church, and to agree together while asking for impossible things. In other words, concentrate on what you *do* know; trust God for the rest.

9

Conclusion

To the Church Leader

In my opinion, a glance through Spirit-filled revival history reveals that leadership has been lacking. As people began to feel new touches or movements of the Spirit, they were also free to express themselves however they desired. Basically, no one mentored them. No one taught them how to manage the line between the Spirit and the emotional, or how to wait until the proper time to share a word. In addition, the fear of quenching the Spirit kept many pastors from training their people in the areas of spiritual gifts and manifestations.

As a result, the modern church has discipleship programs for marriage, prayer, giving, serving, and evangelism, but there has been a tremendous lack of discipleship programs regarding how to operate effectively in spiritual dimensions. This is a tragic oversight. Many good people have been classified as loopy, when they were only immature due to the lack of leadership in their lives. In addition, the move of the Spirit has been thrown out of many churches—again, it's due to a lack of leadership.

Throughout my time in ministry, I've seen many healings and deliverances. My team and I have seen legs grow out, missing organs replaced, ears opened, cancers healed, tumors fall off, billion-dollar financial turnarounds, and marriages restored. At the same time, we've also buried people, prayed with them after their divorces, and stood with them as they've lost their jobs. We've experienced the miraculous, and we've also been disappointed while believing for the miraculous.

I once had a pastor confront me. He told me that I was just getting people's hopes up when it was likely that they would die or not receive the answer to their prayers. First, I'd like to say that it's a compliment to hear that I get people's hopes up. I'd rather be accused of raising their hopes than crushing their spirits. Secondly, when I get to heaven, if God tells me I oversold His love, power, and ability to His people, I'll take the correction from Him then. In the meantime, I'm going to brag on His love, power, and ability. I can also tell you that I *don't* want to get to heaven and find that His people could have experienced so much more if His ministers were only willing to pray big prayers for healing and miracles.

*Jesus said to him, "If you can believe, **all things are possible** to him who believes."*
Mark 9:23 *(emphasis mine)*

The devil cannot stop God, but he *can* stop you from believing God. According to the verse above, all things are possible when we believe, but there has been an attack on the faith of pastors recently. They have begun to pull away from praying for miracles; they fear disappointment. Unfortunately, the world grows us up pretty quickly, and the vicious or immature actions of others can make us pull away from stepping out in faith. However, I believe that these are the reasons that Jesus told us to become like little children again (Matthew 18:3). We are to have childlike faith and a trusting heart that is free of cynicism.

Even so Abraham believed God, and it was reckoned to him as righteousness.
Galatians 3:6, NASB

Abraham believed God. Period. That is where the thought is completed. Abraham didn't believe for righteousness. He didn't believe for healing, prosperity, or long life. He believed God, and that's why he was counted as righteous.

Are we believers who still believe? Do we trust God? Do we trust Him with His Church?

Having the faith of Abraham is merely having faith *in God*. However, it's more than a belief in His existence; it's having faith in Him altogether.

> *But without faith it is impossible to please Him, for he*
> *who comes to God must believe that He is **and** that He is*
> *a rewarder of those who seek Him.*
> **Hebrews 11:6** *(emphasis mine)*

Believing God exists is the first step, but the next step is a belief in His identity. He is a rewarder. He is good. He is love, and everything He does is good. We can trust God, and we can trust His Spirit. We may have been disappointed by unanswered prayer. We may have received prophetic words that never came to pass. We may have tried freedom ministry and remained bound. But we, as leaders and as Spirit-filled people, must come to the decision that we will operate in these gifts and the moves of the Spirit. Why? Because He told us to. We must take all of our questions and concerns to Him and then trust Him with them.

I, also, have had quite the journey with healings and

the gifts of the Spirit. I, like you, have seen the conjured up and emotional moves of people done in the name of the Holy Spirit. I have seen things done in the name of the Spirit that ended up hurting a lot of people.

However, the crux of my journey happened about ten years ago. My wife was pregnant with our first children, twins. The pregnancy was difficult, and she was on bed rest and at home for weeks at a time. She was unable to get up or even do simple things in an effort to protect the babies that were trying to come early. If you know my independent wife, you know how hard all that resting was for her. Then, after six weeks in bed at home, she moved to the hospital for six more weeks of bed rest.

At that time, our church was experiencing a growth spurt; our numbers doubled in one month. I did as much work as possible from her hospital room and ran back to the church for services and meetings. But in spite of everything, the tests and ultrasounds pointed to healthy babies. Then, after weeks of trying to protect our precious babies, the doctors discovered something wrong. Our soon-to-be firstborn, Isaiah, was having a massive brain hemorrhage in the womb.

The news came as a shock. We never expected to hear bad news. We were faith preachers! We believed in miracles and healings!

Not long after, our son was born with level 4 brain

damage. In other words, he was born with cerebral palsy, and there was no explanation for the complication. To make matters worse, the doctors and nurses gave us a very unpromising report. One nurse even told us that he would be completely incapacitated.

I also remember that a woman down the hall was a drug abuser. The authorities were there, ready to take the child from her care as soon as she delivered, and this woman ended up delivering a healthy baby. And while I was relieved that the child next door would have no physical issues, as a human being, I was also angry. I was angry at God. I was angry at the whole situation, and I was preaching on healing that week at church—and here my child was born with brain damage.

In the weeks that followed, the twins grew slowly. My son survived, but the complete and total healing I prayed for did not happen. He went through brain surgery, spinal taps, and many other medical procedures, and I was unable to spare him.

On one of those long hospital days, I sat across from my wife in the hospital cafeteria and told her that I never wanted to preach healing again. I was done with the gifts of the Spirit. I knew that the church could still survive if I just preached morality and playing nice with other people, shared the way to salvation, and never again raised hopes—mine or anyone else's—regarding healing.

My wife, on the other hand, cut right to the point, as she so often does. She looked at me and asked, "What does the Bible say?"

Those five simple words changed my attitude. I knew the Bible said to believe God for miracles. The Bible said, "Is any sick among you? Call for the elders of the church, and the prayer of faith will save the sick" (James 5:14). The Bible said that God is a healer. In the Bible, everyone who came to Jesus for healing was healed. The Bible never said to dissuade hope in healing or in any of God's promises. And it was then that I knew I was called to preach the whole Bible, even if my own experiences didn't make sense.

My son has been a miracle in the making. Some miracles are instant, and some take time. But Isaiah is now ten years old. He doesn't talk, walk, or relate to the world like we do, but he's come so far. They said he was blind, but God has restored his sight. He is also very interactive, and he used to be oblivious to those around him. He has even started to say small words and sentences. In addition, he has increased our lives and our understanding of love and faith. We've also learned how to believe for something over a long period of time.

Now imagine what would have happened had I cut healing from my theology. Weekly, we see healings of all kinds. Weekly, we see testimonies of salvation, baptisms in the Holy Spirit, signs, wonders, and miracles. If I and my team would have stopped moving in the gifts of the Spirit, these hundreds of testimonies may have never occurred. Many people may have stayed in bondage.

No, I don't have answers to everything. We sometimes have amazing nights of healing, and at the end of the night, I still push my son out the door in his wheelchair.

In some ways, this experience has made us "real." We don't come across like we have it all figured out. If we did, everyone would see the results we believe Scripture teaches. Nevertheless, we've made the commitment to keep trying, to keep praying, and to keep laying hands on the people who come through our doors. We were never told to heal people; we were told to lay hands on the sick. God is the one who brings the results. Our job is to give our people the opportunity to hear the Word of God so they can believe.

Don't get me wrong. I still believe for my son's total healing, but I also know how to embrace him just as he is today. There is something so powerful that comes from contentment. We can appreciate where we are in every season, while believing for miracles at the same time.

Please don't let disappointment shape your theology.

A good friend of mine recently used this illustration. In baseball, a great hitter has a batting average of .300. Do you know what that means? It means that three out of ten times at bat, he'll hit the ball. On the other hand, this also means that seven out of ten times, he'll miss the ball. Then again, if he quits swinging, he'll never hit the ball.

If we quit praying, we'll never see a breakthrough. But if we keep "swinging," we're sure to hit something, and we'll also probably learn how to hit it more often. So even though you may have seen spiritual gifts done incorrectly, keep trying. Keep swinging.

What is Revival or a Move of God?

In conclusion, I want to ask, "What is revival?"

Is revival defined by Azusa street, by the manifestation of clouds and flames on buildings? Is revival defined by Toronto, with manifestations and wonders? Is revival defined by Brownsville, with mass salvations and miracles? Is revival on God TV or TBN?

I believe that revival is defined by the salvation of people and by their freedom from all the works of the devil. Revival is people falling totally in love with God. Revival is the children of God genuinely worshipping Him and becoming an active part of the Church and of the mission to reach the lost. Revival is the body of Christ serving their communities, making a difference in culture and in the needs of the community. Revival is all of these things happening on a consistent basis.

We've been trained to think that revival or a move of God is ethereal and sensational, but you may be in the midst of a revival and never even realize it. Sure, you may not have a revival service every night, but every time you gather together, God shows up, moves, saves, and sets free. If your church is taking consistent steps forward for the Kingdom of God, you are in the midst of a revival. You don't need to copy someone else's movement; you need to fan *your* church's movement into a flame.

God is just looking for a people who will yield and let Him lead the way. A Spirit-filled church is a church where the pastor and the people have said yes to God. A Spirit-filled church isn't identified by its banners, shofars, tambourines, or flaming doves. A Spirit-filled church is identified by the testimonies and the fruit of people whose lives have been touched by the Spirit. It's about freedom, wholeness, empowerment, and ministry. It's not about a show, a particular way of service, or a demonstration. A Spirit-filled church is about getting results that blow the enemy away (Acts 1:8).

I challenge you: don't copy our flow or methods. Instead, have a discussion with your leadership about how the Holy Spirit flows in your culture and environment. Where does the book of Acts fit into your context?

Let's train up a generation that knows how to walk in the Spirit effectively in every arena. Let's apply all that we've learned about leadership, guest services, and human nature to all we know about the Holy Spirit. Let's be that two-edged sword of spiritual leadership. Let's be both spiritual and leaders in this world. ❦

About the Author

Kevin and his wife, Maria, are the lead pastors of Life Church in Illinois, USA. They started their church in 2004 with just eighteen people. Today, Life Church is a multi-campus congregation of over thirteen hundred, with a TV ministry and a university level pastoral leadership college.

Kevin and Maria's passion is to raise up Spirit-filled leaders that will plant Spirit-filled churches. They desire to see excellence, relevance and fruitfulness in the life of EVERY Spirit-filled believer.

Find out more at **lifechurchag.com**, and follow Kevin on social media at **@kevinkringel**.

Prayer

We hope you enjoyed this book and that it has been both a blessing and a challenge to your life and walk with God. Maybe you just got hold of it and are glancing through before starting. We made the decision as a publishing company right from the start never to take for granted that everyone has prayed a prayer to receive Jesus as their Lord, so we are including that as the finale to this book. If you have never asked Jesus into your life and would like to do that now, it's so easy. Just pray this simple prayer:

Dear Lord Jesus,
Thank You for dying on the cross for me. I believe
that You gave Your life so that I could have life.
When You died on the cross, You died as an
innocent man who had done nothing wrong. You
were paying for my sins and the debt I could
never pay. I believe in You, Jesus, and receive the
brand new life and fresh start that the Bible

promises that I can have. Thank You for my sins
forgiven, for the righteousness that comes to me
as a gift from You, for hope and love beyond
what I have known and the assurance of eternal
life that is now mine.
Amen.

Good next moves are to get yourself a Bible that is easy to understand and begin to read. Maybe start in John so you can discover all about Jesus for yourself. Start to pray—prayer is simply talking to God—and, finally, find a church that's alive and get your life planted in it. These simple ingredients will cause your relationship with God to grow.

Why not email us and let us know if you did that so we can rejoice with you?

info@greatbiglifepublishing.com

Further Information

For further information about the author of this book, or to order more copies, please contact:

Great Big Life Publishing
Empower Centre
83-87 Kingston Road
Portsmouth
Hampshire
PO2 7DX
United Kingdom
info@greatbiglifepublishing.com

Are you an Author?

Do you have a word from God on your heart that you're looking to get published to a wider audience? We're looking for manuscripts that identify with our own vision of bringing life-giving and relevant messages to Body of Christ. Send yours for review towards possible publication to:

Great Big Life Publishing
Empower Centre
83-87 Kingston Road
Portsmouth
Hampshire
PO2 7DX
United Kingdom
info@greatbiglifepublishing.com